English Grammar for Students of French

The Study Guide for Those Learning French

Seventh edition

Jacqueline Morton

with the collaboration of *Hélène Neu*,
University of Michigan, Ann Arbor

The Olivia and Hill Press®

THE O&H STUDY GUIDES
Jacqueline Morton, editor

English Grammar for Students of Spanish
English Grammar for Students of French
English Grammar for Students of German
English Grammar for Students of Italian
English Grammar for Students of Latin
English Grammar for Students of Russian
English Grammar for Students of Japanese
English Grammar for Students of Arabic
English Grammar for Students of Chinese
Gramática española para estudiantes de inglés

Printed in the U.S.A.

ISBN: 978-0-934034-42-5

Library of Congress Control Number: 2013930691

CONTENTS

CONTENTS

CONTENTS

STUDY TIPS

English Grammar for Students of French (EGSF) is a bridge from
English grammar to French grammar. Once you have learned
a part of speech or a function as it applies to English, it will be
easier for you to understand what is being introduced in your
French textbook.

Each short chapter is divided into two sections, *In English*
and *In French,* both explain the same grammar point and alert
you to the similarities and differences between the two lan-
guages. You will find step-by-step tools to apply grammar rules
and to get from an English structure to a French structure.

To assess your comprehension, you can download a Review
Booklet and Answer Key from www.oliviahill.com. On our site
we can also help you customize *EGFS* to the French textbook
you are using. Just go to *French Correlations*, click on the name
of your textbook and download the pages to be read in *EGSF*
before each lesson.

Note: In keeping with our approach to introduce grammar
from the perspective of the language of today's students, our
examples are based on contemporary spoken English. The
standard written English equivalent is also given to facilitate
the transition to French.

TIPS FOR LEARNING GRAMMAR

Grammar is one of the tools you need to communicate orally
and in writing. Linking a grammar point to its purpose will
make grammar more meaningful and help you recall what you
have learned. Most textbooks indicate the purpose of the
grammar point being introduced either in the title or subtitle
of the grammar section, or within the first paragraph. For
example:

> Title — Descriptive adjectives
>
> Purpose — Describing family and friends

Grammar rules are very useful because they enable a speaker
to generalize. For instance, the grammar rule to add an "s"
when there is more than one object (book vs. book**s**) enables
us to apply it to other words (table vs. table**s**). Without rules,
we'd be forced to memorize every word separately.

1. Reading a grammar rule in your textbook is not sufficient. Make sure that you understand the explanation. Take notes and write a couple of examples to see how they illustrate the rule. If anything is not clear, be sure to ask your teacher at the first opportunity. Clear up problems as early as possible so that you don't fall behind.

2. As you progress in your studies, review previous lessons regularly. To facilitate learning, textbooks tend to focus on one grammar point per section. Bear in mind that these points are not independent; they are part of a whole. In other words, as you learn new rules, don't forget the ones covered in previous lessons.

TIPS FOR LEARNING VOCABULARY

One aspect of language learning is remembering a number of foreign words.

To learn vocabulary — Flashcards are a good, handy tool for learning new words and their meaning. You can carry them with you, group them as you wish, and add information as you advance. Creating your own flashcards is an important first step in learning vocabulary.

1. Write the French word or expression on one side of an index card and its English equivalent on the other side.

2. On the French side add a short sentence using the word or expression. To make sure that your sentence is grammatically correct, copy an example from your textbook substituting the names of people and places with ones you know. It will be easier for you to remember a word in a familiar context. For review purposes, note down the page number of your textbook where the word is introduced.

3. On the French side include any irregularities and whatever information is relevant to the word in question. You will find specific suggestions under the *Study Tips* sections of this handbook.

How to use the cards — Regardless of the side you're working on, always say the French word out loud.

1. Look at the French side first. Going from French to English is easier than from English to French because it only requires your recognizing the French word. Read the French word(s) out loud, giving the English equivalent, then check your answer on the English side.

2. When you go easily from French to English, turn the cards to the English side. Going from English to French is

harder than going from French to English because you have to pull the word and its spelling out of your memory. Say the French equivalent out loud as you write it down, then check the spelling. Some students prefer closing their eyes and visualizing the French word and its spelling.

3. As you progress, put aside the cards you know and concentrate on the ones you still don't know.

How to remember words — Below are suggestions to help you associate a French word with an English word with a similar meaning. This is the first step; it will put the French word in your short-term memory. Use and practice, the next step, will put the words in your long-term memory.

1. There are many words, called COGNATES, that have the same meaning and approximately the same spelling in English as in French. These words are easy to recognize in French, but you will have to concentrate on the differences in spelling and pronunciation.

English	French
activity	activité
music	musique
furious	furieux

2. Try to associate the French word with an English word that has a related meaning.

French	English	Related English word
l'avion	the plane	aviation
beau	handsome	beauty
le vent	the wind	ventilation

3. If the French word has no similarities to English, rely on any association that is meaningful to you. The more associations you have for a word, i.e., the more "hooks," the easier it will be for you to remember it. Different types of associations work for different people. Find the one that works best for you. Here are some suggestions:

   ■ Group words by topics or personal associations — It is easier to learn new words if you group them. You can group them according to topics such as food, clothing, activities you do for fun, sports, school, home, or according to personal associations such as things you carry in your backpack, things you'd take on a desert island, gifts you'd like to receive, etc.

- Associate the word with an image — If you have trouble remembering a particular word, you might want to create a "bizarre image" in your mind with which to associate it.

> **la maison** = *house*
> "She goes to the *house* in **May** with her **son**."
>
> **l'eau** = *water*
> "I jumped into the cold *water* and shouted: "**oh, oh**!!""

4. To reinforce the French word and its spelling, use it in a short sentence.

TIPS FOR LEARNING WORD FORMS

Another aspect of language learning is remembering the various forms a word can take; for example, another form of *book* is *books*, and *play* can take the form of *playing* and *player*. As a general rule, the first part of the word indicates its meaning and the second part indicates its form.

To learn forms — Paper and pencil are the best tools to learn the various forms of a word. You should write them down until you get them right. The following steps will make learning forms easier.

1. Look for a pattern in the different forms of a word.
   - Which letters, if any, remain constant?
   - Which letters change?
   - Is there a pattern to the changes?
   - Is this pattern the same as one you already know?
   - If this pattern is similar to one you already know, what are the similarities and differences?

   We will help you establish patterns in the *Study Tips* following selected chapters.
2. Once you have established the pattern, it will be easy to memorize the forms.
   - Take a blank piece of paper and write down the forms while saying them out loud.
   - Continue until you are able to write all the forms correctly without referring to your textbook.
3. Write short sentences using the various forms.

To review forms — You can use flashcards to review forms. See p. 2 for suggestions on what to write on the cards.

Tips for effective study

Before class — Study the sections in *EGSF* listed in the *French Correlations* (see p. 1) that correspond to the assigned grammar topic. You will learn the relevant grammatical terminology, the similarities and differences between English and French, and how to avoid common pitfalls. Afterwards move on to your textbook. Take notes as you study; highlighting is not sufficient. The more often you write down and use vocabulary and rules, the easier it will be for you to remember them. Good preparation enables you to take advantage of classroom activities.

In class — Take notes. This will remind you what the teacher considers important and will reinforce what you are studying. Focus on developing your communicative skills by practicing the language with your classmates.

Homework — Do the exercises and activities over several short periods of time rather than in one long session. As you write French words or sentences, say them out loud. Each time you write, read, say or hear a word, it is reinforced in your memory. When you correct written exercises, don't erase your errors. Instead, write the correct answer in a different color so you will know what you need to review. Try to figure out why you made the mistake. Refer back to your textbook for help.

Objective — You have learned something successfully when you are able to write a short sentence in French using the correct form of the French words without reference to a textbook or a dictionary. The *Study Tips* throughout this handbook will help you with this process.

We wish to thank Hélène Neu at the University of Michigan, Ann Arbor, for her valuable contribution to this and previous editions. We have profited from her many years of teaching experience and her eagle eye going over the manuscript. We also wish to thank Sabine Gabaron, also at the University of Michigan, who for many years has facilitated the work of teachers and students by correlating *EGSF* to popular first-year college textbooks. This latest edition has benefited from their knowledge of the trends in current French textbooks.

WHAT'S IN A WORD?

1   When you learn a foreign language, in this case French, you
must look at each word in four ways: MEANING, PART OF SPEECH,
FUNCTION, and FORM.

MEANING

An English word may be connected to a French word that
has a similar meaning.

> *Boy*, a young male child, has the same meaning as the French
> word **garçon**.

Words with equivalent meanings are learned by memorizing
10   VOCABULARY (see pp. 2-3).

In addition, every language has expressions in which the
meaning of a group of words is different from the meaning
of the words taken individually. These are called IDIOMATIC
EXPRESSIONS or IDIOMS. For instance, *"to fall* asleep" and *"to
take* a walk" are English expressions where "to fall" and "to
take" do not have their usual meaning as in *"to fall* down the
stairs" or *"to take* a book to school." You will have to be on
the alert for idioms because they cannot be translated word-
for-word in French.

20   *to fall asleep*   s'endormir
[word-for-word *"to put oneself to sleep"*]

to take a walk   faire une promenade
[word-for-word *"to make a walk"*]

PART OF SPEECH

In English and in French words are grouped according to
how they are used in a sentence. There are eight groups corresponding to eight PARTS OF SPEECH:

nouns	articles
verbs	adverbs
pronouns	prepositions
adjectives	conjunctions

30

Some parts of speech are further broken down according to
type. Adjectives, for instance, can be descriptive, interrogative, demonstrative, or possessive. Each part of speech has its
own rules for spelling, pronunciation, and use.

In order to choose the correct French equivalent of an English word, you will have to identify its part of speech. As an example, look at the word *plays* in the following two sentences. In each sentence it belongs to a different part of speech, each one corresponding to a different French word.   40

John *plays* squash.
verb = **joue**

John writes *plays*.
noun = **pièces**

The various sections of this handbook show you how to identify parts of speech so that you are able to choose the proper French words and the rules that apply to them.

FUNCTION

In English and in French the role a word plays in a sentence   50 is called its **FUNCTION**. For example, words that are nouns can have the following functions:

subject
direct object
indirect object
object of a preposition

In order to choose the correct French equivalent of an English word, you will have to identify its function. As an example, look at the word *him* in the following two sentences. In each sentence it has a different function, each one   60 corresponding to a different French word.

Alex sees *him*.
Whom does Alex see? him → direct object → **le**

Alex gives *him* the book.
To whom does Alex give the book? him → indirect object → **lui**

The various sections of this handbook show you how to identify the function of words so that you can to choose the proper French words and the rules that apply to them.

    70

FORM

In English and in French a word can influence the form of another word, that is, its spelling and pronunciation. This "matching" is called **AGREEMENT** and it is said that one word "agrees" with another.

I am   *am* agrees with *I*
she is   *is* agrees with *she*

80 Agreement does not play a big role in English, but it is an important part of the French language. As an example, look at the sentences below where the lines indicate which words must agree with one another.

> *The beautiful white car belongs to my big brother.*

> La belle **voiture** blanche appartient à mon grand **frère**.

In English, the only word that affects another word in the sentence is *car*, which forces us to say *belongs*. If we changed *car* to *cars*, we would have to say *belong* to make it agree with *cars*.

90 In French, the word for *car* (**voiture**) not only affects the spelling and pronunciation of *belongs* (**appartient**), but also of the words for *the* (**la**), *beautiful* (**belle**), and *white* (**blanche**). The word for *brother* (**frère**) affects the spelling and pronunciation of the French words for *my* (**mon**) and *big* (**grand**).

As the various parts of speech are introduced in this handbook, we will go over "agreement" so that you learn which words agree with others and how the agreement is shown.

WHAT IS A NOUN?

A **NOUN** is a word that can be the name of a person, animal, place, thing, event, or idea.

- a person — professor, clown, student, girl
  Julia, Alex, Daniel, Jade
- an animal — dog, bird, bear, snake
  Spot, Tweetie, Teddy
- a place — city, state, country, continent
  stadium, restaurant, France, Europe
- a thing — lamp, airplane, iPad, dress
  Perrier, Eiffel Tower, Arch of Triumph
- an event — graduation, marriage, birth, death
  or activity — football, robbery, rest, growth
- an idea — poverty, democracy, humor, mathematics
  or concept — addition, strength, elegance, virtue

As you can see, a noun is not only a word which names something that is tangible (i.e., that you can touch), such as *lamp, dog*, and *Eiffel Tower,* it can also be the name of things that are abstract (i.e., that you cannot touch), such as *poverty, mathematics,* and *virtue.*

A noun that is not the name of a specific person, place, thing, etc. is called a **COMMON NOUN.** A common noun does not begin with a capital letter, unless it is the first word of a sentence. All the words above that are not capitalized are common nouns.

A noun that is the name of a specific person, place, thing, etc. is called a **PROPER NOUN.** A proper noun always begins with a capital letter. All the words above that are capitalized are proper nouns.

Julia is a singer.
proper   common
noun   noun

A noun that is made up of two words is called a **COMPOUND NOUN.** A compound noun can be composed of two nouns, such as *comic strip* and *ice cream.*

IN ENGLISH

To help you learn to recognize nouns, look at the paragraph below where the nouns are in *italics*.

> The best *products* from *France* include *wines, perfumes, scarves, gloves,* and other luxury *items.* Today, French *workers* make excellent *skis* and *tennis rackets* that are sold the *world* over. Thanks to the *European Union,* you can find *goods* from *Germany, Italy, England,* and their commercial *partners* in all large French *stores.* Thus, Italian *sports cars,* English *leather,* German *glassware,* and Belgian *lace* can be bought at *prices* comparable to those in the *country* of *origin.*

IN FRENCH

Nouns are identified in the same way as they are in English.

TERMS USED TO TALK ABOUT NOUNS

- GENDER — A noun has a gender; that is, it can be classified according to whether it is masculine, feminine, or neuter (see *What is Meant by Gender?*, p. 11).
- NUMBER — A noun has a number; that is, it can be classified according to whether it is singular or plural (see *What is Meant by Number?*, p. 14).
- COUNT OR NON-COUNT — A noun can be classified as to whether it is a count noun or non-count noun; that is, whether it refers to something that can be counted or not (see p. 20 in *What is an Article?*).
- FUNCTION — A noun can have a variety of functions in a sentence; that is, it can be the subject of the sentence (see *What is a Subject?*, p. 29) or an object (see *What is an Object?*, p. 111).

STUDY TIPS — NOUNS AND THEIR GENDER (SEE P. 21)

WHAT IS MEANT BY GENDER?

GENDER in the grammatical sense means that a word can be classified as masculine, feminine, or neuter.

> Did Roger give Alice the book?
> Yes, *he* gave *it* to *her.*
> | | |
>   masc.   neuter fem.

Gender is not very important in English; however, it is at the very heart of the French language where the gender of a word is often reflected not only in the way the word itself is spelled and pronounced, but also in the way all the words connected to it are spelled and pronounced.

In French, each part of speech follows its own rules to indicate gender. You will find gender discussed in the chapters dealing with articles and the various types of pronouns and adjectives. In this section we shall only look at the gender of nouns (see *What is a Noun?*, p. 9).

IN ENGLISH

Nouns themselves do not have a gender, but sometimes their meaning indicates a gender based on the biological sex of the person or animal the noun stands for. For instance, when we replace a proper or common noun that refers to a man or a woman, we use *he* for males and *she* for females.

■ nouns referring to males indicate the MASCULINE gender

> Roger came home; *he* was tired, and I was glad to see *him.*
> | | |
> noun (male)   masculine   masculine

■ nouns referring to females indicate the FEMININE gender

> Alice came home; *she* was tired, and I was glad to see *her.*
> | | |
> noun (female)   feminine   feminine

Proper or common nouns that do not have a biological gender are considered NEUTER and are replaced by *it.*

> Paris is a lovely city. I enjoyed visiting *it.*
> | | |
> noun   noun   neuter

IN FRENCH

All nouns — common nouns and proper nouns — have a gender; they are either masculine or feminine. Do not confuse the grammatical terms "masculine" and "feminine" with the terms "male" and "female." Only a few French nouns have a grammatical gender tied to whether they refer to someone of the male or female sex, most nouns have a gender that must be memorized.

The gender of common and proper nouns based on BIOLOGICAL GENDER is easy to determine. These are nouns whose meaning can only refer to one or the other of the biological sexes, male or female.

MALES → MASCULINE	FEMALES → FEMININE
Alex	Julia
boy	girl
brother	sister
son	daughter

The gender of other nouns, common and proper, cannot be explained or figured out. These nouns only have a GRAMMATICAL GENDER that is unrelated to biological sex and that must be memorized. Here are some examples of English nouns classified under the gender of their French equivalent.

MASCULINE	FEMININE
boat	car
suicide	death
Japan	France
computer	video

As you learn a new noun, you should always learn its gender because it will affect the spelling and pronunciation of the words related to it. Textbooks and dictionaries usually indicate the gender of a noun with an *m.* for masculine or an *f.* for feminine. Sometimes indefinite articles are used: *un* for masculine or *une* for feminine (see *What is an Article?*, p. 16).

Here is a list of some noun endings that often, but not always, indicate a noun's gender:

MASCULINE

-age	avantage, garage, bagage
-eau	chapeau *(hat)*, manteau *(coat)*, cadeau *(gift)*
-et	objet, sujet, secret
-isme	capitalisme, impressionnisme, tourisme
-ment	gouvernement, monument, événement *(event)*
-oir	miroir *(mirror)*, soir *(evening)*, couloir *(hallway)*

FEMININE

-ace/	glace *(ice cream)*, place, surface
-asse	impasse *(cul-de-sac)*, classe
-aison	maison *(house)*, saison *(season)*, comparaison
-ance/	tolérance, assurance *(insurance)*, substance
-ence	présence, absence, compétence
-ade	promenade *(walk)*, escapade, ambassade
-esse	promesse *(promise)*, adresse, richesse
-ette	cassette, bicyclette, serviette *(napkin)*
-ière	lumière *(light)*, bière *(beer)*, manière *(manner)*
-sion/	télévision, décision, profession, compréhension
-tion	nation, production, compétition
-té	société, liberté, nationalité, beauté *(beauty)*
-tude	étude *(study)*, attitude, solitude
-ure	ceinture *(belt)*, aventure, nature, peinture *(painting)*

80

90

CAREFUL — Do not rely on noun endings to determine a noun's grammatical gender as there are many exceptions. Always check the gender in your textbook or the dictionary. Also, do not rely on biological gender to indicate the grammatical gender of French nouns that can refer to a man or a woman. For instance, the grammatical gender of the noun **personne** *(person)* is always feminine, even though it can refer to a man.

STUDY TIPS — NOUNS AND THEIR GENDER (SEE P. 21)

CHAPTER

4

WHAT IS MEANT BY NUMBER?

1   **NUMBER** in the grammatical sense means that a word can be classified as singular or plural. When a word refers to one person or thing, it is said to be **SINGULAR**; when it refers to more than one, it is **PLURAL**.

one *book*   two *books*
    | |
singular   plural

More parts of speech indicate number in French than in English and there are more spelling and pronunciation changes in French than in English.

10

ENGLISH	**FRENCH**
nouns	nouns
verbs	verbs
pronouns	pronouns
demonstrative adjectives	adjectives
	articles

Since each part of speech follows its own rules to indicate number, you will find number discussed in the chapters dealing with articles, the various types of adjectives and pronouns, as well as in all the sections on verbs. In this section we shall only
20   look at the number of nouns.

IN ENGLISH

A singular noun is made plural in one of two ways:

1. some singular nouns add an *"-s"* or *"-es"*

book	book**s**
kiss	kiss**es**

2. other singular nouns change their spelling

man	men
mouse	mice
leaf	leaves
child	children

30

Some nouns, called **COLLECTIVE NOUNS**, refer to a group of persons or things, but the noun itself is considered singular.

The *team* has eleven players.
The *family* is well.

IN FRENCH

As in English, the plural form of a noun is usually spelled differently than the singular form.

The most common change is the same as the one made in English; that is, an "**-s**" is added to the singular masculine or feminine noun.

	SINGULAR	PLURAL		
MASCULINE	livre	livres	*book*	*books*
FEMININE	table	tables	*table*	*tables*

Some nouns indicate the plural differently. When that is the case, your textbook will give you the plural form.

As in English, French collective nouns are considered singular.

L'équipe a onze joueurs.
The team has eleven players.
　　 singular

La famille va bien.
The family is well.
　　 singular

Your textbook will give you additional rules for nouns that form their plural differently, for instance, singular nouns ending in **-al** → **-aux**: journ**al** → journ**aux** *(newspaper, newspapers)*.

HEARING THE PLURAL

In English you can usually hear the plural in the noun itself.

SINGULAR	PLURAL
the *book*	the *books*
the *child*	the *child**ren***

In French, even though you can see the plural ending, you often don't hear it in the noun itself because the final "s" is not pronounced.

same pronunciation

livre	livre**s**
enfant	enfant**s**

In that case, to know whether a noun is singular or plural, you listen to the words before the noun, such as **le** and **la** for the singular or **les** for the plural (see *What is an Article?*, p. 16).

SINGULAR	PLURAL
le livre	**les** livres
l'enfant	**les** enfants

40

50

60

70

WHAT IS AN ARTICLE?

1   An **ARTICLE** is a word placed before a noun to show whether the noun refers to a specific person, animal, place, thing, event, or idea, or whether it refers to a non-specific person, thing, or idea.

> I saw *the* boy you spoke about.
> a specific boy

> I saw *a* boy in the street.
> not a specific boy

10   In English and in French there are two types of articles, **DEFINITE ARTICLES** and **INDEFINITE ARTICLES**.

DEFINITE ARTICLES
IN ENGLISH

A **DEFINITE ARTICLE** is used before a noun when we are referring to a specific person, place, animal, thing, or idea. There is one definite article, ***the***.

> Give me *the* book on the table.
> a specific book

20

> I ate *the* apple from the garden.
> a specific apple

The definite article remains *the* even when the noun that follows becomes plural.

> Give me *the books* on the table.
> I ate *the apples* from the garden.

IN FRENCH

As in English, a definite article is used before a French noun when referring to a specific person, place, animal, thing, or

30   idea.

> Donne-moi **le** livre sur la table.
> *Give me **the** book on the table.*
> J'ai mangé **la** pomme du jardin.
> *I ate **the** apple from the garden.*

Unlike in English, however, there is more than one definite article. In French, the definite article works hand-in-hand with the noun to which it belongs in that it matches the noun's gender and number. This "matching" is called AGREEMENT. One says that "the article *agrees* with the noun" (see *What is Meant by Gender?*, p. 11 and *What is Meant by Number?*, p. 14).

A different article is used, therefore, depending on whether the noun is masculine or feminine (gender) and on whether the noun is singular or plural (number).

There are four forms of the definite article: three singular forms and one plural form.

- **le** indicates that the noun is masculine singular

      le livre   *the book*
      le garçon   *the boy*

- **la** indicates that the noun is feminine singular

      la table   *the table*
      la pomme   *the apple*

- **l'** is used instead of **le** and **la** before a word beginning with a vowel.[1] It does not indicate if the noun is masculine or feminine.

      l'étudiant   *the student*
      |
      masculine

      l'université   *the university*
      |
      feminine

Since the letter "h" is never pronounced in French, a word starting with "h" is usually considered as beginning with a vowel and uses **l'** as a definite article: **l'hiver** *(the winter)*; **l'hôtel** *(the hotel)*. Your textbook will go into the few exceptions to this rule.

- **les** is used to indicate that the noun is plural. Since there is only one form, it does not indicate if the noun is masculine or feminine.

      les livres   *the books*
      les tables   *the tables*

You will often have to rely on the different forms of articles to indicate the gender and number of the noun (see p. 15 regarding the "hearing" of the plural in French).

---

[1]Vowels are the sounds associated with the letters *a, e, i (y), o* and *u;* consonants are the sounds associated with the other letters of the alphabet.

CAREFUL — French nouns often require the use of a definite article when none is expressed in English. Here are some examples.

- when the noun is used to speak in general terms

80
> *I like* **chocolate.**
> J'aime **le chocolat.**
>
> **Elephants** *are strong.*
> **Les éléphants** *sont forts.*

- when the noun refers to a concept

> **Time** *is* **money.**
> **Le temps,** *c'est de* **l'argent.**
>
> **Goodness** *is worth more than* **beauty.**
> **La bonté** vaut mieux que **la beauté.**

90
- the names of countries and geographical areas

la France	*France*
le Portugal	*Portugal*
l'Allemagne	*Germany*
le Texas	*Texas*

Consult your textbook for exceptions and for more details on the use of definite articles in French.

INDEFINITE ARTICLES
IN ENGLISH

100
An **INDEFINITE ARTICLE** is used before a noun when we are not referring to a specific person, animal, place, thing, event, or idea. There are two indefinite articles, *a* and *an*.

- *a* is used before a word beginning with a consonant

> I saw *a* boy in the street.
> not a specific boy

- *an* is used before a word beginning with a vowel

> I ate *an* apple.
> not a specific apple

110
The indefinite article is used only with a singular noun. To indicate a non-specific plural noun, the word *some* or *any* can be used, but it is usually left out.

> I ate apples.
> I ate *(some)* apples.
>
> Do you have brothers and sisters?
> Do you have *(any)* brothers and sisters?

IN FRENCH

As in English, an indefinite article is used before a French noun when referring to a non-specified person, place, animal, thing, or idea. Just as with French definite articles, indefinite articles must agree with the noun's gender and number. There are three forms of the indefinite article: two singular forms and one plural form.

- **un** indicates that the noun is masculine singular

un livre	*a book*
un garçon	*a boy*

- **une** indicates that the noun is feminine singular

une table	*a table*
une pomme	*an apple*

- **des** is used to indicate that the noun is plural. Since there is only one form, it does not indicate if the noun is masculine or feminine. Unlike English where the plural definite article *some* can be omitted, the French equivalent **des** must be expressed.

des livres	*some books*
des tables	*some tables*

  J'ai mangé **des** pommes.
  *I ate (**some**) apples.*

The three forms above, **un**, **une**, and **des**, usually change to **de** when the verb is negated (see *What are Affirmative and Negative Sentences?*, p. 49).

j'ai **un** livre → je n'ai pas **de** livres
*I have **a** book* → *I don't have **a** book*

j'ai **une** table → je n'ai pas **de** table
*I have **a** table* → *I don't have **a** table*

j'ai **des** pommes → je n'ai pas **de** pommes
*I have (**some**) apples* → *I don't have **any** apples*

Consult your textbook for exceptions and for more details on the use of indefinite articles in French.

CAREFUL —Work on the assumption that all French nouns are preceded by an article of one sort or another. It is an exception when they are not.

NON-COUNT NOUNS AND PARTITIVE ARTICLES
IN ENGLISH

160   Common nouns can be divided into two groups: count nouns as opposed to non-count nouns.

COUNT NOUNS — As the name implies, count nouns designate objects that can be counted; for example, you can count the noun *pen: one pen, two pens....* Count nouns can be singular or plural. (On the preceding pages all the examples used for indefinite articles are count nouns.)

NON-COUNT NOUNS — As the name implies, non-count nouns designate objects that cannot be counted; for example, you cannot count the noun *water: one water, two waters....* Non-

170   count nouns are always singular.

    In English, it is usually not important to distinguish between count and non-count nouns since they both use the same articles. In French, however, it is important to identify non-count nouns.

IN FRENCH

    Non-count nouns do not use indefinite articles, instead they use a set of articles called **PARTITIVE ARTICLES.** These articles only have a singular form for each gender since non-count

180   nouns are always singular. Unlike in English where *some* or *any* can be omitted, the French partitive articles must be expressed.

- **du** is used before a masculine non-count noun

    J'achète **du** beurre.
    *I am buying (**some**) butter.*

    Avez-vous **du** beurre?
    *Do you have (**any**) butter?*

- **de la** is used before a feminine non-count noun

190   J'achète **de la** viande.
    *I am buying (**some**) meat.*

    Avez-vous **de la** viande?
    *Do you have (**any**) meat?*

- **de l'** replaces **du** and **de la** before a non-count noun beginning with a vowel. It does not indicate if the noun is masculine or feminine.

    Je bois **de l'**eau.
           feminine
    *I am drinking (**some**) water.*

Devez-vous **de** l'argent?   200
|
masculine
*Do you owe **(any)** money?*

The above is a brief summary of partitive articles. Refer to
your textbook for rules regarding their usage.

STUDY TIPS — NOUNS AND THEIR GENDER

Flashcards (see *Tips for Learning Vocabulary*, p. 2)
1. Make a flashcard for each new noun, listing the singular, and the plural
   if it is irregular, on the French side.
2. Use blue cards or blue pen for masculine nouns and red cards or red pen
   for feminine nouns. Associating the noun with blue or red will help you
   remember its gender.
3. Precede the noun with the appropriate definite article: **le, la** or
   l' (masc.) or **l'** (fem.).
4. Whether you're looking at the English or French side, as you say the
   French noun and article add an adjective such as "intéressant" (*interesting*) whose pronunciation changes according to whether it accompa-
   nies a masculine or feminine noun (in the masculine form the final "t"
   is not pronounced, in the feminine form it is). The change in pronunciation of the adjective will reinforce the noun's gender in your memory.

   le livre (intéressant)   *the (interesting) book*
   la maison (intéressante)   *the (interesting) house*
   l'année (fem.) (intéressante)   *the (interesting) year*

5. Don't forget that it is only by repeated use that you will remember the
   words and their gender.

CHAPTER

6

WHAT IS THE POSSESSIVE?

1   The term **POSSESSIVE** means that one noun owns or *possesses* another noun.

> Julia's French book is on the table.
> possessor   possessed

> The tree's branches are broken.
> possessor   possessed

IN ENGLISH

There are two possessive constructions.

10   1. with an apostrophe

In this structure, the possessor comes before the possessed.

- singular possessor adds an apostrophe + "s"

  Jade's dress
  a tree's branches
  singular possessor

- plural possessor ending with "s" adds an apostrophe after the "s"

  the students' teacher
20   the girls' club
  plural possessor

- a plural possessor not ending with "s" adds an apostrophe + "s"

  the children's playground
  the men's department
  plural possessor

2. with the word *of*

In this structure, the possessed comes before the possessor.

30   - a singular or plural possessor is preceded by *of the* or *of a*

  the book *of the* professor
  the branches *of a* tree
  singular possessor

  the teacher *of the* students
  plural possessor

IN FRENCH

There is only one possessive construction, the "of" structure (2 above). The apostrophe structure (1 above) does not exist. 40

The French structure parallels the English structure: the noun possessed + **de** *(of)* + definite or indefinite article + the common noun possessor (see *What is an Article?*, p. 16). If the possessor is a proper noun there is no preceding article.

Jade's dress	la robe **de** Jade
possessor possessed	possessed possessor
proper noun	*the dress of Jade*

the professor's book	le livre **du** professeur
possessor possessed	**de + le** 50
common noun	*the book of the professor*

the woman's purse	le sac **de la** dame
	the purse of the lady

a tree's branches	les branches **d'un** arbre
	the branches of a tree

the students' teacher	le professeur **des** étudiants
	de + les
	the professor of the students
60

CAREFUL — Do not confuse **du, de la, de l'**, and **des** used to show possession with words of the same spelling that are indefinite and partitive articles meaning *some* or *any* (pp. 19-20). When they come between two nouns they usually indicate possession: ***the book** of the **teacher*** → **le livre** du **professeur.** Otherwise they are articles: *he eats bread* → Il mange **du** pain.

In English and in French possession can also be indicated using possessive adjectives, i.e., *my dress, his book* → **ma** robe, **son** livre (see *What is a Possessive Adjective?*, p. 94). 70

CHAPTER

7

WHAT IS A VERB?

A **VERB** is a word that indicates the action of the sentence. The word "action" is used in its broadest sense, not necessarily physical action.

Let us look at different types of words that are verbs:

- a physical activity   to run, to hit, to talk, to walk
- a mental activity   to hope, to believe, to imagine, to dream, to think
- a condition   to be, to feel, to have, to seem

Many verbs, however, do not fall neatly into one of the above three categories. They are verbs nevertheless because they represent the "action" of the sentence.

The book *costs* only $5.00.
        to cost

The students *seem* tired.
      to seem

The verb is the most important word in a sentence. You cannot write a **COMPLETE SENTENCE**, that is, express a complete thought, without a verb.

It is important to identify verbs because the function of words in a sentence often depends on their relationship to the verb. For instance, the subject of a sentence is the word doing the action of the verb and the object is the word receiving the action of the verb (see *What is a Subject?*, p. 29, and *What is an Object?*, p. 111).

IN ENGLISH

To help you learn to recognize verbs, look at the paragraph below where verbs are in *italics*.

The three students *entered* the restaurant, *selected* a table, *hung* up their coats, and *sat* down. They *looked* at the menu and *asked* the waitress what she *recommended*. She *suggested* the daily special, beef stew. It *was* not expensive. They *chose* a bottle of red wine and *ordered* a salad. The service *was* slow, but the food *tasted* very good. Good cooking, they *decided, takes* time. They *ate* pastry for dessert and *ended* the meal with coffee. They *felt* happy!

IN FRENCH

Verbs are identified the same way as they are in English.

TERMS USED TO TALK ABOUT VERBS

- **INFINITIVE OR DICTIONARY FORM** — The verb form that is the name of the verb is called an infinitive: *to eat, to sleep, to drink* (see *What is the Infinitive?*, p. 26). In the dictionary a verb is listed without the "to": *eat, sleep, drink.*
- **CONJUGATION** — A verb is conjugated or changes form to agree with its subject: *I do, he does* (see *What is a Verb Conjugation?*, p. 38).
- **TENSE** — A verb indicates tense; that is, the time (present, past, or future) of the action: *I am, I was, I will be* (see *What is Meant by Tense?*, p. 55).
- **MOOD** — A verb shows mood; that is, the speaker's attitude toward what he or she is saying (see *What is Meant by Mood?*, p. 77).
- **VOICE** — A verb shows voice; that is, the relationship between the subject and the action of the verb (see *What is Meant by Active and Passive Voice?*, p. 165).
- **PARTICIPLE** — A verb may be used to form a participle: *writing, written; singing, sung* (see *What is a Participle?*, p. 60).
- **TRANSITIVE OR INTRANSITIVE** — A verb can be classified as transitive or intransitive depending on whether or not the verb can take a direct object (see p. 111 in *What is an Object?*).

CHAPTER

8

WHAT IS THE INFINITIVE?

1 The INFINITIVE form is the name of the verb.

The French equivalent of the verb *to learn* is **étudier.**
<u>   </u>
infinitive

IN ENGLISH

The infinitive is composed of two words: *to* + the dictionary form of the verb *(to speak, to dance)*. By DICTIONARY FORM we mean the form of the verb that is listed as the entry in the dictionary *(speak, dance)*.

Although the infinitive is the most basic form of the verb,
10 it can never be used in a sentence without another verb which is conjugated (see *What is a Verb Conjugation?*, p. 38).

To learn is exciting.
<u>   </u> |
infinitive   conjugated verb

It *is* important *to be* on time.
| <u>   </u>
conjugated verb   infinitive

Alex and Jade *want* *to dance* together.
| <u>   </u>
conjugated verb   infinitive

20 The dictionary form of the verb, rather than the infinitive, is used after a verb such as *must, let,* and *can.*

Alex *must be* home by noon.
|
dictionary form

Mr. Smith *lets* his daughter *watch* television.
|
dictionary form

IN FRENCH

The infinitive form is usually shown by the last two or three letters of the verb called THE ENDING, known as "LA TERMI-
30 NAISON."

danser   *to dance*
finir   *to finish*
vendre   *to sell*

The infinitive form is important not only because it is the form under which a verb is listed in the dictionary, but because the ending often indicates the pattern the verb will follow to create its various forms (see *How to conjugate a verb*, p. 42).

1ˢᵗ CONJUGATION — verbs ending in -**er** follow one pattern
2ᴺᴰ CONJUGATION — verbs ending in -**ir** follow another pattern
3ᴿᴰ CONJUGATION — verbs ending in -**re** follow another pattern   40

CONSULTING THE DICTIONARY

In English it is possible to change the meaning of a verb by placing short words (prepositions or adverbs) after it.

For example, the verb *look* in Column A below changes meaning depending on the word that follows it *(to, after, for, into)*. In French, it is impossible to change the meaning of a verb by adding a preposition or an adverb as in Column A. An entirely different French verb corresponds to each meaning.

COLUMN A		MEANING	FRENCH
to look	→	to look at	**regarder**
		I *looked at* the photo.	
to look *for*	→	to search for	**chercher**
		I *am looking for* a book.	
to look *after*	→	to take care of	**surveiller**
		I *am looking after* the children.	
to look *into*	→	to study	**étudier**
		We'll *look into* the problem.	

50

CAREFUL — When consulting an English-French dictionary, all   60 the examples under Column A can be found under the dictionary entry *look* (**regarder**); however, you will have to search under that entry for the specific expression *look for* (**chercher**), or *look after* (**surveiller**), to find the correct French equivalent. Don't select the first entry under *look* and then add on the French equivalent for *after, for, into,* etc.; the result will be meaningless in French.

STUDY TIPS — VERBS

Flashcards (see *Tips for Learning Vocabulary*, p. 2)

1. Create flashcards indicating the infinitive form of the French verb on one side and its English equivalent on the other. You might want to select a particular color for verb cards so that later when you add information on the cards you can easily sort them out from the other cards (see Study Tips — *Verb Conjugations*, p. 43; *Tenses,* p. 56; *Le Passé Composé*, p. 68; *The Future Tense*, p. 74).

    finir   *to finish*

2. If the verb is a reflexive verb, indicate "**se**" before the infinitive (see *What are Reflexive Pronouns and Verbs?*, p. 131). If the verb can be used as a reflexive verb and as a non-reflexive verb, write both.

se coucher	*to go to bed*
Je **me couche** tôt.	*I go to bed early.*
coucher	*to put to bed*
Je **couche** les enfants.	*I'm putting the children to bed.*

3. If the verb is followed by the preposition "à" or can be part of a special construction, indicate it on the card with an example.

répondre (à + person/thing)	*to answer*
Je **réponds** à Marc.	*I'm answering Marc.*
Je **réponds au** téléphone.	*I'm answering the phone.*
dire (**à** + person + **de** + infinitive)	*to tell someone to do something*
Marc dit **à** Pierre **de** partir.	*Marc tells Peter to leave.*

Practice

Follow the *Tips for Learning Vocabulary,* p. 2 to learn the French equivalent of English verbs. The real practice will come, however, when you learn to conjugate the verb and use the conjugated forms in sentences.

WHAT IS A SUBJECT?

In a sentence the person or thing that performs the action of the verb is called the **SUBJECT**. To find the subject of a sentence, always look for the verb first, then ask *who?* or *what?* before the verb (see *What is a Verb?*, p. 24). The answer will be the subject.[1]

> *Daniel* speaks French.
>> Verb: speaks
>> Who speaks French? Answer: Daniel.
>> The subject refers to one person; it is singular (p. 14).
>
> Daniel's *books* cost a lot of money.
>> Verb: cost
>> What costs a lot of money? Answer: books.
>> The subject refers to more than one thing; it is plural (p. 14).

If a verb has more than one subject, the subject is considered plural.

> *The book* and *the pencil* are on the table.
>> Verb: are
>> What is on the table? Answer: the book and the pencil.
>> The subject refers to more than one thing; it is plural.

If a sentence has more than one verb, you have to find the subject of each verb.

> *The boys* are cooking while *Alice* sets the table.
>> Boys is the plural subject of *are*.
>> Alice is the singular subject of *sets*.

IN ENGLISH

Always ask *who?* or *what?* before the verb to find the subject. Never assume that the first word in the sentence is the subject. Subjects can be located in several different places, as you can see in the following examples (the ***subject*** is in boldface and the *verb* italicized).

> Did ***the game*** *start* on time?
> After playing for two hours, ***Alex*** *became* exhausted.
> Alice's ***brothers*** from Chicago *arrived* yesterday.
> Here comes ***the boy***.

---

[1]The subject performs the action in an active sentence, but is acted upon in a passive sentence (see *What is Meant by Active and Passive Voice?*, p. 165).

34 **IN FRENCH**

The subject of a sentence is identified the same way as it is in English. Also, as in English, it can be located in different places in the sentence.

CAREFUL — In English and in French it is important to find the subject of each verb to make sure that the verb form agrees with the subject (see *What is a Verb Conjugation?*, p. 38).

WHAT IS A PRONOUN?

A **PRONOUN** is a word used to replace one or more nouns. Therefore, it may stand for a person, animal, place, thing, event, or idea. For instance, rather than repeating the proper noun "Julia" in the following two sentences, it can be replaced by a pronoun in the second sentence.

> *Julia* likes to swim. *Julia* practices every day.
> *Julia* likes to swim. *She* practices every day.

The word that the pronoun replaces or refers to is called the **ANTECEDENT** of the pronoun. In the example above, the pronoun *she* refers to the proper noun *Julia*. *Julia* is the antecedent of the pronoun *she*.

There are different types of pronouns, each serving a different function and following different rules. Listed below are the more important types and the chapters in which they are discussed.

PERSONAL PRONOUNS — These pronouns replace nouns referring to persons or things which have been previously mentioned. A different set of pronouns is often used depending on the pronoun's function in the sentence.

- as subject (see p. 33)

> *I* go; *they* read; *he* runs; *she* sings.

- as direct object (see p. 116)

> Roger loves *it*. Alice met *him*.

- as indirect object (see p. 119)

> Alice gave *us* the book. Speak to *them*.

- as object of a preposition (see p. 127)

> Roger is going out with *her*.

- as a disjunctive (see p. 125)

> Who is there? *Me*.

REFLEXIVE PRONOUNS — These pronouns refer back to the subject of the sentence (see p. 131).

> I cut *myself*. We washed *ourselves*. Alice dressed *herself*.

INTERROGATIVE PRONOUNS — These pronouns are used to ask questions (see p. 140).

> *Who* is that? *What* do you want?

DEMONSTRATIVE PRONOUNS — These pronouns are used to point out persons or things (see p. 160).

> *This (one)* is expensive. *That (one)* is cheap.

POSSESSIVE PRONOUNS — These pronouns are used to show possession (see p. 135).

> Whose book is that? *Mine. Yours* is on the table.

RELATIVE PRONOUNS — These pronouns are used to introduce relative clauses (see p. 148).

> The man *who* came is very nice.
> Where is the book *that* you read last summer?

INDEFINITE PRONOUNS — These pronouns are used to refer to unidentified persons or things.

> *One* doesn't do that.
> *Something* is wrong.

French indefinite pronouns correspond in usage to their English equivalents. They can be studied in your textbook.

IN ENGLISH
Each type of pronoun follows a different set of rules.

IN FRENCH
As in English, each type of pronoun follows a different set of rules. Moreover, French pronouns usually agree in gender and number with their antecedent (see *What is Meant by Gender?*, p. 11, and *What is Meant by Number?*, p. 14).

WHAT IS A SUBJECT PRONOUN?

A **SUBJECT PRONOUN** is a word that replaces a noun and that func-   1
tions as a subject of a verb (see *What is a Subject?*, p. 29).

> *He* worked while *she* read.
>> Who worked? Answer: He.
>> *He* is the subject of the verb *worked*.
>> Who read? Answer: She.
>> *She* is the subject of the verb *read*.

Pronouns which refer to human beings or things are divided
into three groups: 1ˢᵗ, 2ⁿᵈ, and 3ʳᵈ person. The word **PERSON** in
this instance does not necessarily mean a human being; it is a
grammatical term which can refer to any noun.   10

IN ENGLISH

Here is a list of English subject pronouns grouped according
to the person to which they belong.

1ˢᵗ PERSON

I → the person speaking → **SINGULAR**
we → the person speaking plus others → **PLURAL**
> *Julia and I* are free this evening. *We* are going out.

2ⁿᵈ PERSON

you → the person or persons spoken to → **SINGULAR** or **PLURAL**   20
> *Julia*, do *you* sing folk songs?
> *Daniel, Alex, and Julia*, do *you* sing folk songs?

3ʳᵈ PERSON

he, she, it → the person or object spoken about → **SINGULAR**
they → the persons or objects spoken about → **PLURAL**
> Where is the book? *It* is on the table.
> *Alice and Alex* are free this evening. *They* are going out.

IN FRENCH

French subject pronouns are also grouped by person. They   30
are presented in the following order:

SINGULAR

1ˢᵗ PERSON	I	**je**
2ⁿᵈ PERSON	you	**tu**
3ʳᵈ PERSON	he	**il**
	she	**elle**
	it	**il** or **elle**
	(see p. 36)	**on**

Pᴌᴜʀᴀʟ

1ˢᵀ PERSON	we	**nous**
2ᴺᴰ PERSON	you	**vous**
3ᴿᴰ PERSON	they	**ils** or **elles**

As you can see above, there are English subject pronouns which have more than one equivalent in French: *you* (**tu** or **vous**), *it* (**il** or **elle**), *we* (**nous** or **on**), and *they* (**ils** or **elles**). Let us look at each of these pronouns.

"YOU" (2ⁿᵈ person singular and plural)

tu (2ⁿᵈ person familiar singular) or
vous (2ⁿᵈ person formal to address one or more persons)
     (2ⁿᵈ person familiar plural)

IN ENGLISH

The subject pronoun "you" is used when you are speaking to one or more than one person.

> Alice, are *you* coming with me?
> Alice and Daniel, are *you* coming with me?

The same pronoun "you" is used to address the President of the United States or your dog.

> Do *you* have any questions, Mr. President?
> *You* are a good dog, Heidi.

IN FRENCH

When you are speaking to one person there are two forms, depending on the person you're speaking to and whether or not you are on familiar terms with him or her.

- When speaking to a child, an animal, a family member, a friend, or anyone with whom you are on familiar terms, use the FAMILIAR FORM → "TU" (2ⁿᵈ person singular).

> *Mom, are **you** coming with us?*
> |
>   **tu**

- When speaking to a person with whom you are not on familiar terms, use the FORMAL FORM → "VOUS" (2ⁿᵈ person plural). Notice that this formal form is used to address one person.

> *Mrs. Smith, are **you** coming with us?*
> |
>   **vous**

If you are speaking to an adult and unsure which form to use, it is preferable to use **vous**.

- When speaking to more than one person whether you are on familiar terms with them or not, there is only one form → **"vous"** (2nd person plural).

> *Mom and Dad, are **you** coming with us?*
> vous

> *Mr. and Mrs. Smith, are **you** coming with us?*
> vous

"IT" (3rd person singular)

il (3rd person singular masculine) or
elle (3rd person singular feminine)

IN ENGLISH
The subject pronoun "it" is used whenever you are speaking about one thing.

> Where is the book? *It* is on the table.

IN FRENCH
The subject pronoun used depends on the gender of its ANTECEDENT, that is, the noun it replaces.

- masculine antecedent → **il**

> Où est le livre? **Il** est sur la table.
> masc. sing. masc. sing.
> antecedent pronoun
> *Where is the book? It is on the table.*

- feminine antecedent → **elle**

> Voici la chaise. **Elle** est confortable.
> fem. sing. fem. sing.
> antecedent pronoun
> *Here is the chair. It is comfortable.*

"WE" (1st person plural)

nous (1st person plural) or
on (3rd person singular)

IN ENGLISH
The subject pronoun "we" is used when you are speaking about yourself and one or more other persons.

> Daniel and I are students; *we* study a lot.
> I studied with friends; *we* passed the exam.

IN FRENCH

The subject pronoun used is either the 1st person plural pronoun **nous** or, primarily in spoken French, the 3rd person singular pronoun **on**. Depending on which of these two pronouns is used, the verb form will be in either in the 1st person plural when the subject is **nous** or in the 3rd person singular when the subject is **on** (see p. 40 in *What is a Verb Conjugation?*).

> *We study a lot.*
> **Nous étudions** beaucoup.
> └─────────┘
> 1st pers. pl.
>
> **On étudie** beaucoup.
> └────────┘
> 3rd pers. sing.

Consult your textbook for other usages of the pronoun **on**, remembering that regardless of its English equivalent the French verb is always in the 3rd person singular.

"THEY" (3rd person plural)

> **ils** (3rd person plural masculine) or
> **elles** (3rd person plural feminine)

IN ENGLISH

The subject pronoun "they" is used when you are speaking about more than one person or thing.

> Paul and John are students; *they* study a lot.
> Where are the books? *They* are on the table.

IN FRENCH

The subject pronoun used depends on the gender of its ANTECEDENT, that is, the noun it replaces.

- masculine antecedent → **ils**

> Où sont les livres? **Ils** sont sur la table.
>   └──┘   └┘
>   masc. pl.   masc. pl.
>   antecedent pronoun
> *Where are the books? They are on the table.*

> Alex et Roger sont étudiants; **ils** étudient beaucoup.
> └──────────┘   └┘
> 2 masc. sing.   masc. pl.
> antecedents   pronoun
> *Alex and Roger are students. They study a lot.*

> Où sont le livre et le cahier? **Ils** sont sur la table.
>   └──────────────┘   └┘
>   2 masc. sing.   masc. pl.
>   antecedents   pronoun
> *Where are the book and the notebook? They are on the table.*

- feminine antecedent → **elles**

  Voici les chaises; **elles** sont confortables.

  fem. pl.   fem. pl.
  antecedent   pronoun

  *Here are the chairs; **they** are comfortable.*

  Julia et Jade sont étudiantes; **elles** étudient beaucoup.

  2 fem. sing.   fem. pl.
  antecedents   pronoun

  *Julia and Jade are students. **They** study a lot.*

  170

  Où sont la clé et la montre? **Elles** sont sur la table.

  2 fem. sing.   fem. pl.
  antecedents   pronoun

  *Where are the key and the watch? **They** are on the table.*

- antecedents of different genders → **ils**

  Voici la clé et le cahier. **Ils** sont sur la table.

  fem. sing. + masc. sing. → masc. pl.
  antecedents   pronoun

  *Here are the key and the notebook. **They** are on the table.*

STUDY TIPS — SUBJECT PRONOUNS

Flashcards
Create a flashcard for each subject pronoun (1st, 2nd, and 3rd person singular and plural). You'll add the other forms of the pronoun when you learn them (see *Study Tips — Direct and Indirect Object Pronouns*, p. 124).

je	*I*
il	*he, it*

Practice
You'll practice subject pronouns when you practice conjugating verbs (see *Study Tips — Verb Conjugations*, p. 43).

CHAPTER

12

WHAT IS A VERB CONJUGATION?

1   A VERB CONJUGATION is a list of the six possible forms of the verb for a particular tense. For each tense, there is one verb form for each of the pronouns used as the subject of the verb (see *What is Meant by Tense?*, p. 55).

> I am
> you are (one person)
> he, she, it is
> we are
> you are (two+ persons)
> they are

10   Different tenses have different verb forms, but the principle of conjugation remains the same. In this chapter all our examples are in the present tense (see *What is the Present Tense?*, p. 58).

IN ENGLISH

The verb *to be* is the English verb that changes the most; it has three forms: *am, are,* and *is.* (The initial vowel is often replaced by an apostrophe: *I'm, you're, he's.*) Other English verbs only have two forms: *to sing,* for instance.

SINGULAR

1ST PERSON	I *sing*	
2ND PERSON	you *sing*	
3RD PERSON	he *sings* / she *sings* / it *sings*	

PLURAL

1ST PERSON	we *sing*
2ND PERSON	you *sing*
3RD PERSON	they *sing*

Because English verbs change so little, it isn't necessary to learn "to conjugate a verb;" that is, to list all its possible forms. For most verbs, it is much simpler to say that the verb adds an "-s" in the 3rd person singular (see p. 33).

IN FRENCH

Unlike in English, French verb forms change from one person to another so that when you learn a new verb you must also learn how to conjugate it. First, you must establish whether the verb is regular or irregular.

- Verbs whose forms follow a pattern are called REGULAR VERBS. Only one example must be memorized and the pattern can then be applied to other verbs in the same group.
- Verbs whose forms do not follow a pattern are called IRREGULAR VERBS and must be memorized individually. Unfortunately, this is the case of the most commonly used French verbs.

The forms of a verb, whether regular or irregular, are memorized with subject pronouns and the verb form that agrees with that subject pronoun (see *What is a Subject Pronoun?*, p. 33). The listing of subject pronouns and corresponding verb form is referred to as the conjugation, "LA CONJUGAISON," of the verb.

CHOOSING THE PROPER "PERSON" (see p. 33)

Below is the conjugation of the regular verb **chanter** *(to sing)*. Notice that each of the six persons has its own ending and that different pronouns belonging to the same person have the same verb form. For instance, the 3rd person singular has three possible subject pronouns, **il, elle, on**, but they have the same verb form: **chante.**

SINGULAR

1ST PERSON	**je** chante	*I sing*
2ND PERSON	**tu** chantes	*you sing*
3RD PERSON	**il** chante	*he sings, it sings*
	elle chante	*she sings, it sings*
	on chante	*we sing* (see p. 36)

PLURAL

1ST PERSON	**nous** chantons	*we sing*
2ND PERSON	**vous** chantez	*you sing*
3RD PERSON	**ils** chantent	*they sing*
	elles chantent	*they sing*

To choose the proper verb form, you must identify the person (1st, 2nd, or 3rd) and the number (singular or plural) of the subject.

1ST PERSON SINGULAR — The subject is always **je** *(I)*.

Le matin **je chante** bien.
*In the morning **I sing** well.*

2ND PERSON SINGULAR — The subject is always **tu** *(informal you)*.

Daniel, **tu chantes** bien.
*Daniel, **you sing** well.*

3ᴿᴰ PERSON SINGULAR — The subject can be expressed in one of four ways:

80

1. a proper noun

Jade chante bien.

fem. sing. → **elle** *(she)*

Jade sings well.

Alex chante bien.

masc. sing. → **il** *(he)*

Alex sings well.

> In both sentences the proper noun could be replaced by the pronoun *she* (**elle** → fem.) or *he* (**il** → masc.), so you must use the 3ʳᵈ person singular form of the verb.

90

2. a singular common noun

La fille chante bien.

fem. sing. → **elle** *(she)*

The girl sings well.

L'oiseau chante bien.

masc. sing. → **il** *(it)*

The bird sings well.

> In both sentences the common noun could be replaced by the pronoun *she* (**elle** → fem.) or *it* (**il** → masc.), so you must use the 3ʳᵈ person singular form of the verb.

100

3. the 3ʳᵈ person singular masculine pronoun **il** *(he, it)* or the 3ʳᵈ person singular feminine pronoun **elle** *(she, it)*

Alex aime chanter. **Il chante** bien.

masc. sing.   masc. sing.

*Alex likes to sing. **He sings** well.*

Regardez ce livre. **Il est** intéressant.

masc. sing. masc. sing.

*Look at this book. **It is** interesting.*

110

Jade aime chanter. **Elle chante** bien.

fem. sing.   fem. sing.

*Jade likes to sing. **She sings** well.*

Voici la chaise. **Elle est** confortable.

fem. sing. fem. sing.

*Here is the chair. **It is** comfortable.*

4. the 3ʳᵈ person singular pronoun **on** *(we, see p. 36)*

On chante bien.

3ʳᵈ pers. sing.

120

We sing well.

1ˢᵀ PERSON PLURAL — The subject can be expressed in one of
two ways:

1. a multiple subject in which the speaker is included

> **Jade, Alex et moi chantons** bien.
> ‾‾‾‾‾‾‾‾‾‾‾‾‾‾‾‾
>   **nous**
>
> *Jade, Alex and I sing well.*
>
> > The subject, *Jade, Alex,* and *I,* could be replaced by the pronoun
> > *we,* so you must use the 1ˢᵗ person plural form of the verb.

2. the first person plural pronoun **nous** *(we)*   130

> **Nous chantons** bien.
> *We sing well.*

2ᴺᴰ PERSON PLURAL — The subject is always **vous** *(you,* see
pp. 34-5).

> Monsieur et Madame Dupont, **vous chantez** bien.
> *Mr. and Mrs. Dupont, you sing well.*
>
> Madame Dupont, **vous chantez** bien.
> *Mrs. Dupont, you sing well.*

3ᴿᴰ PERSON PLURAL — The subject can be expressed in one of   140
three ways:

1. a plural noun

> **Les filles chantent** bien.
> |
>   fem. pl. → **elles** *(they)*
> *The girls sing well.*

2. two or more proper or common nouns

> **Julia et Jade chantent** bien.
> ‾‾‾‾‾‾‾‾‾‾‾‾‾
>   fem. + fem. → **elles** *(they)*
> *Julia and Jade sing well.*   150
>
> **La fille et le garçon chantent** bien.
> ‾‾‾‾‾‾‾‾‾‾‾‾‾‾‾‾‾‾
>   fem. + masc. → **ils** *(they)*
> *The girl and the boy sing well.*

3. the 3ʳᵈ person plural masculine pronoun **ils** *(they)* or the 3ʳᵈ
person plural feminine pronoun **elles** *(they)*

> **Alex et Daniel aiment** chanter. **Ils chantent** bien.
> ‾‾‾‾‾‾‾‾‾‾‾‾‾‾‾ |
>   masc. + masc. → **ils** *(they)*   masc. pl.
> *Alex and Daniel like to sing. They sing well.*
>   160
> Regardez ces livres. **Ils sont** intéressants.
> | |
>   masc. pl. masc. pl.
> *Look at these books. They are interesting.*

Julia et Jade aiment chanter. **Elles chantent** bien.

fem. + fem. → **elles** *(they)*   fem. pl.

Julia and Jade like to sing. They sing well.

Voici les chaises. **Elles sont** confortables.

fem. pl.   fem. pl.

Here are the chairs. They are comfortable.

HOW TO CONJUGATE A VERB

A French verb, whether regular or irregular, is composed of two parts:

1. the STEM or ROOT, "LA RACINE," is found by dropping the last two letters from the infinitive (see *What is the Infinitive?,* p. 26).

INFINITIVE	STEM
chanter	chant-
finir	fin-
vendre	vend-

The stem of regular verbs usually remains the same throughout a conjugation. You will have to memorize the changes in the stem of irregular verbs.

2. the ENDING, "LA TERMINAISON," changes for each person in the conjugation of regular and irregular verbs.

Regular verbs are divided into three GROUPS, also called CONJUGATIONS, identified by the last two letters of the infinitive ending of the verb.

-er	-ir	-re
1ˢᵗ group	2ⁿᵈ group	3ʳᵈ group

Each of the three verb groups has its own set of endings for each tense (see *What is Meant by Tense?,* p. 55). Memorizing the conjugation of one sample verb for each tense of each group enables you to conjugate in the various tenses the other regular verbs belonging to that group.

As an example of the steps to follow to conjugate a regular verb, let us look at verbs of the 1ˢᵗ group (**-er** verbs); that is, verbs like **parler** *(to speak)* and **aimer** *(to love)* that follow the pattern of **chanter** *(to sing)* conjugated on p. 39.

1. Identify the group of the verb by its infinitive ending.

parler
aimer   →1ˢᵗ conjugation or group

2. Find the verb stem by removing the infinitive ending.

> parl-
> aim-

3. Add the ending that agrees with the subject.

je parle	j'aime
tu parles	tu aimes
il parle	il aime
elle parle	elle aime
on parle	on aime
nous parlons	nous aimons
vous parlez	vous aimez
ils parlent	ils aiment
elles parlent	elles aiment

210

The endings of regular verbs belonging to the other groups are different, but the process of conjugation is the same. Just follow the three steps above.

220

As irregular verbs are introduced in your textbook, their entire conjugation will be given so that you can memorize them individually. Be sure to do so because the most frequently used verbs are irregular: **être**, *to be;* **avoir**, *to have;* **aller**, *to go;* **faire**, *to make.*

CAREFUL — French verb forms are often pronounced the same way, but written differently (for instance, *parle, parles, parlent*). The only way to write the proper ending of a verb is to identify its subject.

STUDY TIPS — VERB CONJUGATIONS

(see *Tips for Learning Word Forms*, p. 4)

REGULAR -ER VERBS

Pattern — As in all regular verbs, the stem usually remains the same throughout the conjugation; only the endings change according to the subject.

Look at the conjugation of **jouer** *(to play)*:

je joue	nous jouons
tu joues	vous jouez
il/elle/on joue	ils/elles jouent

Regular -er verbs have the same boot pattern: all the forms inside the boot have the same pronunciation. As you learn new verbs and conjugations, see if the pattern fits into a boot. If it does, it will be easier to memorize.

Practice

1. When you learn the conjugation of a verb, write down the different forms as many times as you need to so that you can do it without referring to your textbook. Since many verb forms have the same pronunciation, be sure to link the spelling of each ending with its subject.
2. Apply the pattern you've just learned to another regular –er verb.
3. Write your own sentences using the different forms of different regular –**er** verbs.
4. Practice using the various forms out of order so that when you speak you don't have to go through the entire conjugation.
5. Do all the exercises in your textbook and workbook only after you've understood the explanations and examples in your textbook, taken notes, and gone through steps 1 through 4 above. Do not refer to the textbook as you're doing the exercises; consider them as a self-test to measure what you have learned. When you've finished all the exercises on your own, go back to the textbook to correct your mistakes. Use a colored pen for corrections so that the errors stand out when you review.

Flashcards

Take out the flashcards you created to learn the meaning of verbs (see p. 27) and add the following information on the French side:

■ Indicate that the verb is regular.

  parler (reg.)   *to speak*

■ Indicate any irregularity in the stem.

  manger   *to eat*
  nous mangeons *we eat*

REGULAR -IR VERBS

Pattern — As in all regular verbs, the stem usually remains the same throughout the conjugation; only the endings change according to the subject.

Look at the conjugation of **finir** (*to finish*):

je fin**is**	nous fin**issons**
tu fin**is**	vous fin**issez**
il/elle/on fin**it**	ils/elles fin**issent**

Regular -**ir** verbs have the same vertical pattern: all the singular forms on the left have the same pronunciation and all the plural forms on the right include an "ss" in the spelling and the"s" sound in pronunciation.

As you learn new conjugations, always look for similarities and differences with a conjugation you've already learned. It will make it easier for you to know which forms to concentrate on and how to distinguish between conjugations. In the case of regular -**ir** verbs, compare the endings to those of the same subject of regular -**er** verbs. To highlight the differences, we've put them in **bold** below:

	-er	**-ir**
je	-e	-s
tu	-es	-s
il/elle/on	-e	-t
nous	-ons	-issons
vous	-ez	-issez
ils/elles	-ent	-issent

Practice and flashcards

See suggestions for regular **-er** verbs on previous page.

IRREGULAR VERBS

Pattern — As in all irregular verbs, the stem as well as the endings can change throughout the conjugation.

1. Start by looking for a pattern within the conjugation of the irregular verb.
   - stem — look for similarities in the various forms
   - endings — look for similarities with verbs you've already learned.

   For example, let's look at the irregular verb **boire** *(to drink)*.

je **bois**	nous buvons
tu **bois**	vous buvez
il/elle/on **boit**	ils/elles **boivent**

Stem — There is a boot pattern similar to regular **-er** verbs. There is also a vertical pattern similar to regular **-ir** verbs.
- all the stems except for **nous** and **vous** start with **boi-**
- the stems of **nous** and **vous** start with **bu-**
- all the plural stems have a "**v**"

Endings — Although the endings change, there are similarities with the endings of regular verbs.
- the singular forms have the same endings as regular **-ir** verbs
- the plural forms have the same endings as regular **-er** verbs

CAREFUL — There are verbs that do not fit in either the boot or vertical pattern. You will have to look for a pattern, if there is one.

Practice and flashcards

See suggestions for regular **-er** verbs above. On the flashcard be sure to indicate when the verb is irregular.

boire (irreg.)   *to drink*

CHAPTER

13

WHAT IS AN AUXILIARY VERB?

1 A verb is called an AUXILIARY VERB or HELPING VERB when it helps
another verb, called the MAIN VERB, form one of its tenses.

He *has been* gone two weeks.	*has*	AUXILIARY VERB
	been	AUXILIARY VERB
	gone	MAIN VERB

IN ENGLISH

There are three verbs that can be used as auxiliary verbs, *to
have, to be,* and *to do*, as well as a series of auxiliary words
such as *will, would, may, must, can, could*, that are used to
10 change the tense and meaning of the main verb.

- Auxiliaries are used primarily to indicate the tense of the
main verb (present, past, future — see *What is Meant by
Tense?*, p. 55).

Julia *is* reading a book.   PRESENT
auxiliary *to be*

Julia *has* read a book.   PAST
auxiliary *to have*

Julia *will* read a book.   FUTURE
20 auxiliary *will*

- The auxiliary verb *to do* is used to help formulate questions
and to make sentences negative (see *What are Declarative
and Interrogative Sentences?*, p. 52, and *What are Affirmative
and Negative Sentences?*, p. 49).

Does Julia *read* a book?   INTERROGATIVE SENTENCE
Julia *does not* read a book.   NEGATIVE SENTENCE

IN FRENCH

30 There are only two auxiliary verbs: **avoir** (*to have*) and **être**
(*to be*). They are used to change the tense of the main verb.

The other English auxiliaries such as *do, does, did, will*, or
would do not exist as auxiliaries in French. Their meaning is
conveyed either by a different structure or by a form of the
main verb. You will find more on this subject under the
chapters dealing with the different tenses.

The verbs **avoir** and **être** are irregular verbs whose conjugations must be memorized. They are important verbs because they serve both as auxiliary verbs and main verbs.

J'**ai** ce livre. *I **have** that book.*	**avoir** *(to have)*	MAIN VERB
J'**ai acheté** ce livre. *I **bought** that book.*	**avoir** acheter *(to buy)*	AUXILIARY VERB MAIN VERB
Je **suis** à la maison. *I **am** at home.*	**être** *(to be)*	MAIN VERB
Je **suis allé** à la maison. *I **went** home.*	**être** aller *(to go)*	AUXILIARY VERB MAIN VERB

A verb tense composed of an auxiliary verb plus a main verb is called a **COMPOUND TENSE**, as opposed to a **SIMPLE TENSE** that is a tense composed of only the main verb.

Je **mange.**
simple tense
present of **manger**
I eat.

J'**ai mangé.**
auxiliary   main
verb   verb
compound tense
past tense of **manger**
I have eaten.

AUXILIARY VERBS ARE USED TO INDICATE TENSE

Verbs take either **avoir** or **être** as auxiliary to form all of their compound tenses (see p. 64 for guidelines on selecting the proper auxiliary). The auxiliary, conjugated in the different tenses, plus the past participle of the main verb form the various tenses of the main verb (see p. 61 in *What is a Participle?*).

Let us look at examples of some compound tenses. The first sentence of each pair has a verb that takes a form of **avoir** as auxiliary (**manger**, *to eat*) and the second sentence has a verb that takes a form of **être** as auxiliary (**aller**, *to go*).

PASSÉ COMPOSÉ (PRESENT PERFECT) — Present of **avoir** or **être** + past participle of main verb (see *What is the Past Tense?*, p. 63). Notice that there are two possible English equivalents.

Le garçon **a mangé** la pomme.
*The boy **ate (has eaten)** the apple.*

La fille **est allée** au cinéma.
*The girl **went (has gone)** to the movies.*

80 **PLUS-QUE-PARFAIT (PAST PERFECT)** — Imperfect of **avoir** or **être** + past participle of main verb (see *What is the Past Perfect Tense?*, p. 69).

> Le garçon **avait mangé** la pomme.
> *The boy **had eaten** the apple.*

> La fille **était allée** au cinéma.
> *The girl **had gone** to the movies.*

FUTUR ANTÉRIEUR (FUTURE PERFECT) — Future of **avoir** or **être** + past participle of main verb (see *What is the Future Perfect* 90 *Tense?*, p. 75).

> Le garçon **aura mangé** la pomme.
> *The boy **will have eaten** the apple.*

> La fille **sera allée** au cinéma.
> *The girl **will have gone** to the movies.*

CONDITIONNEL PASSÉ (PAST CONDITIONAL) — Conditional of **avoir** or **être** + past participle of main verb (see p. 82 in *What is the Conditional?*).

> Le garçon **aurait mangé** la pomme.
100 > *The boy **would have eaten** the apple.*

> La fille **serait allée** au cinéma.
> *The girl **would have gone** to the movies.*

You will learn other compound tenses as your study of French progresses.

WHAT ARE AFFIRMATIVE AND NEGATIVE SENTENCES?

A sentence can be classified according to whether it states that 1
something is true or that something is not true.

An AFFIRMATIVE SENTENCE is a sentence that states a positive fact.

France *is* a country in Europe.
Roger *will work* at the university.
They *liked* to travel.

A NEGATIVE SENTENCE is a sentence that states a fact that is denied.

France *is not* a country in Asia.
Roger *will not* work at the university.
They *did not like* to travel.

IN ENGLISH   10

An affirmative sentence can be made negative in one or two
ways:

1. by adding **not** after an auxiliary verb or an auxiliary word
   (see *What is an Auxiliary Verb?*, p. 46)

AFFIRMATIVE	NEGATIVE
Roger *is* a student.	Roger *is not* a student.
Alice *can* do it.	Alice *cannot* do it.
They *will* travel.	They *will not* travel.

   The word *not* is often attached to the auxiliary and the letter
   "o" is replaced by an apostrophe; this is called a CONTRACTION: 20
   is not → isn't; cannot → can't; will not → won't.

2. by adding the auxiliary verb **do, does,** or **did + not,** and
   giving the dictionary form of the main verb

AFFIRMATIVE	NEGATIVE
We *study* a lot.	We *do not study* a lot.
Alice *writes* well.	Alice *does not write* well.
The train *arrived.*	The train *did not arrive.*

   Frequently, *do, does,* or *did* is contracted with *not: do not →*
   don't; does not → doesn't; did not → didn't.
                                                                     30
IN FRENCH

An affirmative sentence is made negative by putting **ne (n'**
before a vowel) right after the subject and the negative **pas**
(not) after the conjugated verb.

AFFIRMATIVE
Elles **mangent** beaucoup.
They eat a lot.

NEGATIVE
Elles **ne** mangent **pas** beaucoup.
                    conjugated verb
They do not eat a lot.

Marie **écrit** bien.
Mary writes well.

Marie **n'**écrit **pas** bien.
                conjugated verb
Marie does not write well.

Le train **est** arrivé.
The train arrived.

Le train **n'**est **pas** arrivé.
                conjugated verb
The train did not arrive.

CAREFUL — Remember that there is no equivalent for the auxiliary words *do, does, did* in French; do not try to include them in negative sentences.

NEGATIVE WORDS
In English and in French there are other negative words besides *not* (**ne...pas**).

IN ENGLISH
There are two sets of negative words: those that are used in affirmative sentences and their equivalents used in negative sentences. Here are the most common negative words.

NEGATIVE WORD IN AFFIRMATIVE SENTENCE	NEGATIVE WORD IN NEGATIVE SENTENCE
never	ever
no longer	any longer
no more	any more
nobody	anybody
no one	anyone
nothing	anything

Let's look at some examples

■ *never, ever*
   I *never* eat after midnight.
   I *don't ever* eat after midnight.

■ *no longer (no more), any longer (anymore)*
   We will *no longer* travel.
   We won't travel *any longer*.

■ *nobody (no one), anybody (anyone)*
   Before the exam he sees *nobody (no one)*.
   Before the exam he *doesn't* see *anybody (anyone)*.

■ *nothing, anything*
   I have *nothing* to give you.
   I *don't* have *anything* to give you.

IN FRENCH

Unlike in English, there is only one set of negative words. The most common are **jamais** *(never, ever)*, **plus** *(no longer, no more, any longer, anymore)*, **personne** *(nobody, anybody)*, and **rien** *(nothing, anything)*.

In most instances the placement of these negative words is the same as that of the negative word **pas**, i.e. after the conjugated verb.

Never, ever → **ne ... jamais**

> Je **ne** dors **jamais** dans l'avion.
> *I **never** sleep on a plane.*
> *I **don't** ever sleep on a plane.*

No longer, no more, any longer, anymore → **ne ... plus**

> Je **ne** vais **plus** en vacances.
> *I **no longer** go on vacation.*
> *I **don't** go on vacation **anymore**.*

Nobody anybody (**personne**) *and nothing, anything* (**rien**)

- subject of a sentence → **personne/rien + ne**

> Personne **ne** part en vacances.
> ***Nobody (no one)** is going on vacation.*

> Rien **n**'est gratuit.
> ***Nothing** is free.*

- object of a verb in a simple tense → **ne ... personne /rien**

> Il **ne** voit **personne**.
> *He sees **nobody (no one)***
> *He **doesn't** see **anybody**.*

> Je **ne** vois **rien**.
> *I see **nothing**.*
> *I **don't** see **anything**.*

- **rien** object of a verb in a compound tense → **ne** + auxiliary verb + **rien** + past participle

> Je **n**'ai **rien** vu.
> *I saw **nothing**.*
> *I **didn't** see **anything**.*

- **personne** object of a verb in a compound tense → **ne** + auxiliary verb + past participle + **personne**

> Je **n**'ai vu **personne**.
> *I saw **no one**.*
> *I **didn't** see **anybody**.*

The above is an introduction to negative words and their placement. We refer you to your textbook for additional information.

CHAPTER

15

WHAT ARE DECLARATIVE AND
INTERROGATIVE SENTENCES?

A sentence can be classified as to whether it is making a statement or asking a question.

A **DECLARATIVE SENTENCE** is a sentence that makes a statement.

> Columbus discovered America in 1492.

An **INTERROGATIVE SENTENCE** is a sentence that asks a question.

> Did Columbus discover America in 1492?

In written language, an interrogative sentence always ends with a question mark.

IN ENGLISH

A declarative sentence can be changed to an interrogative sentence in one of two ways:

1. by adding the auxiliary verb *do, does,* or *did* before the subject and using the dictionary form of the main verb

DECLARATIVE SENTENCE	INTERROGATIVE SENTENCE
Alex *likes* the class.	*Does* Alex *like* the class?
Alex and Jade *sing* well.	*Do* Alex and Jade *sing* well?
Alice *went* to Paris.	*Did* Alice *go* to Paris?

2. by inverting the normal word order of subject + verb to verb + subject. This **INVERSION** can only be used with auxiliary verbs or auxiliary words (see *What is an Auxiliary Verb?*, p. 46).

DECLARATIVE SENTENCE	INTERROGATIVE SENTENCE
Alex is home.	*Is Alex* home?
You have received a letter.	*Have you received* a letter?
She will come tomorrow.	*Will she come* tomorrow?

IN FRENCH

A declarative sentence can be changed to an interrogative sentence in one of two ways:

1. by adding the expression **est-ce que** before the complete declarative sentence

> **Est-ce que** je peux manger maintenant?
> | I can eat now |
>
> complete declarative sentence
>
> *Can I eat now?*

> **Est-ce que** Jade mange à la maison?
> *Jade eats at home*
> complete declarative sentence
> *Does Jade eat at home?*

2. by using the inversion form

- when the subject is a pronoun (except for the subject pronoun **je** which can only use the expression **est-ce que**), invert the verb and pronoun subject

> **Vous mangez** à la maison ce soir.
> **Mangez-vous** à la maison ce soir?
> *You are eating at home this evening.*
> *Are you eating at home this evening?*

- when the subject is a noun, construct the question as follows:
  1. State the noun subject.
  2. State the verb and, when writing, add a hyphen.
  3. State the subject pronoun that corresponds to the gender and number of the subject (see pp. 33-7).

Let's look at a few examples.

> **Daniel est-il** à la maison?
> (word-for-word: *Daniel is he home*)
> Noun subject **Daniel** → masc. sing. → pronoun masc. sing. → **il**
> *Is Daniel home?*

> **La montre et la clé sont-elles** sur la table?
> (word-for-word: *the watch and the key are they on the table*)
> Two noun subjects, **la montre** and **la, clé** both fem. sing.
> → pronoun fem. pl. → **elles**
> *Are the watch and the key on the table?*

> **Daniel et Alice étudient-ils** ensemble?
> (word-for-word: *Daniel and Alice do they study together*)
> Two noun subjects **Daniel** → masc. sing. and **Alice** → fem. sing.
> → pronoun masc. pl. → **ils** (see p. 37).
> *Do Daniel and Alice study together?*

When a verb ending with a vowel in the 3rd person singular is inverted, **-t-** is added between the verb and subject pronoun to facilitate pronunciation.

> Daniel **aime-t-il** ses cours à l'université?
> *Does Daniel **like** his classes at the university?*

> Alice **va-t-elle** manger au restaurant?
> *Is Alice **going** to eat at the restaurant?*

Consult your textbook for more information.

CAREFUL — When *do, does,* or *did* are used as auxiliaries make sure that you do not translate them. Just like the expression **est-ce que**, they are used to turn the complete sentence which follows into a question.

TAG QUESTIONS

In English and in French, when you expect a yes-or-no answer, you can also transform a statement into a question by adding a short phrase at the end of the statement. This short phrase is called a TAG.

IN ENGLISH

There are many different tags, depending on factors such as the tense of the verb in the statement and whether the statement is affirmative or negative. For instance, affirmative statements take negative tags and negative statements take affirmative tags (see *What are Affirmative and Negative Sentences?*, p. 49).

> Daniel and Alice *study* together, *don't they?*
> Daniel and Alice *don't study* together, *do they?*

IN FRENCH

There is only one tag, **n'est-ce pas?** It can be added to any statement requiring a yes-or-no answer to turn it into a question.

> Daniel et Alice étudient ensemble, **n'est-ce pas?**
> *Daniel and Alice study together, **don't they?***

> Daniel et Alice n'étudient pas ensemble, **n'est-ce pas?**
> *Daniel and Alice don't study together, **do they?***

WHAT IS MEANT BY TENSE?

The TENSE of a verb indicates when the action of the verb takes
place: at the present time, in the past, or in the future. The
word *tense* comes from the same word as the French word
"temps," which means *time*.

I am eating.	PRESENT
I ate.	PAST
I will eat.	FUTURE

As you can see in the above examples, just by putting the verb
in a different tense and without giving any additional information, ex. I am eating *now*, I ate *yesterday*, I will eat *tomorrow*, you
can indicate when the action of the verb takes place.

Tenses may be classified according to the way they are
formed. A SIMPLE TENSE consists of only one verb form, ex. I *ate*,
while a COMPOUND TENSE consists of one or more auxiliaries plus
the main verb, ex. I *am eating*, he *has been eating* (see *What is an
Auxiliary Verb?*, p. 46).

In this section we will only consider tenses of the indicative
mood (see *What is Meant by Mood?*, p. 77).

IN ENGLISH

Listed below are the main tenses of the indicative mood
whose equivalents you will encounter in French.

PRESENT

I study	PRESENT
I do study	PRESENT EMPHATIC
I am studying	PRESENT PROGRESSIVE

PAST

I studied	SIMPLE PAST
I did study	PAST EMPHATIC
I have studied	PRESENT PERFECT
I had studied	PAST PERFECT
I was studying	PAST PROGRESSIVE

FUTURE

I will study	FUTURE
I will have studied	FUTURE PERFECT

As you can see, there are only two simple tenses, present and
simple past; all the other tenses are compound tenses.

IN FRENCH

Listed below are the main tenses of the indicative mood that you will encounter in French.

40

PRESENT

| j'étudie | I study, I am studying, I do study | PRÉSENT (PRESENT) |

PAST

j'ai étudié	I studied, I have studied, I did study	PASSÉ COMPOSÉ (PRESENT PERFECT)
j'étudiais	I was studying, I used to study	IMPARFAIT (IMPERFECT)
j'avais étudié	I had studied	PLUS-QUE-PARFAIT (PAST PERFECT)

FUTURE

50

| j'étudierai | I will study | FUTUR (FUTURE) |
| j'aurai étudié | I will have studied | FUTUR ANTÉRIEUR (FUTURE PERFECT) |

As you can see, there are more simple tenses in French than in English: present, imperfect, future. French compound tenses are formed with the auxiliary verbs **avoir** *(to have)* or **être** *(to be)* + the past participle of the main verb (see p. 61 in *What is a Participle?*). The verb **étudier** above uses the auxiliary verb **avoir** to form its compound tenses.

This handbook discusses the various tenses and their usage in separate chapters: *What is the Present Tense?*, p. 58; *What is the Past Tense?*, p. 63; *What is the Past Perfect Tense?*, p. 69; *What is the Future Tense?*, p. 72, and *What is the Future Perfect Tense?*, p. 75. Verb tenses can be grouped according to the mood to which they belong (see *What is Meant by Mood?*, p. 77).

60

CAREFUL — Do not assume that tenses with the same name in English and in French are used in the same way.

STUDY TIPS — TENSES

Pattern (see *Tips for Learning Word Forms*, p. 4)
1. Start by comparing the forms of the new tense to the other forms of that verb you already know, particularly the forms that are close in spelling and/or pronunciation.
   - Identify the similarities with the other tenses. This will help you remember the new tense.
   - Identify the differences with the other tenses. This will help you avoid mixing them up.
2. Remember that a verb that is irregular in one tense is not necessarily irregular in another.

Practice

1. To learn the forms of a simple tense, follow the instructions *Study Tips — Verb conjugations*, p. 43.
2. To learn the forms of a compound tense, follow the instructions *Study Tips —* **Le passé composé**, p. 68.
3. Apply the pattern you've just learned by writing and saying aloud another verb that follows the same pattern.
4. Rewrite the practice sentences of a tense you've learned earlier using the new tense.

Flashcards

As you learn new tenses, sort out the verbs from your other cards and note any irregularities on the French side.

vouloir	*to want* (infinitive, see *Study Tips,* p. 27)
je veux	*I want*
nous voulons	*we want*
ils veulent	*they want* (present, see *Study Tips,* p. 45)
j'ai voulu	*I wanted to , I tried to* + infinitive (***passé composé***, see *Study Tips,* p. 68)
voudr-	(stem future/conditional see *Study Tips,* p. 74)

As you learn more verbs and tenses, you will be able to recognize more patterns and will have to write less on the card.

CHAPTER

17

WHAT IS THE PRESENT TENSE?

1   The PRESENT TENSE indicates that the action of the verb is happening at the present time. It can be at the moment the speaker is speaking, a habitual action, or a general truth.

> I *see* you.
> He *smokes* constantly.
> The sun *rises* every day.

IN ENGLISH

There are three forms of the verb that indicate the present tense. Each form has a slightly different meaning:

10

> Mary *studies* in the library.   PRESENT
> Mary *is studying* in the library.   PRESENT PROGRESSIVE
> Mary *does study* in the library.   PRESENT EMPHATIC

Depending on the way a question is worded, you will automatically choose one of the three above forms in your answer.

> Where does Mary study? She *studies* in the library.
> Where is Mary now? She *is studying* in the library.
> Does Mary study in the library? Yes, she *does [study* in the library].

20

IN FRENCH

The present tense, "LE PRÉSENT," is a simple tense formed by adding a set of endings to the stem of the verb. Your textbook will give you the present tense endings of regular verbs of the various conjugations and of irregular verbs (see *What is a Verb Conjugation?*, p. 38).

Unlike in English, there is only one verb form to indicate the present tense. The French present tense is used to express the meaning of the English present, present progressive, and
30   present emphatic tenses.

> *Mary **studies** in the library.*
> |
>   étudie
>
> *Mary **is studying** in the library.*
> |_____|
>   étudie
>
> *Mary **does study** in the library.*
> |_____|
>   étudie

CAREFUL — Since the French present tense is always indicated by the ending of the verb, without an auxiliary verb such as *is* and *does*, you must not translate these English auxiliary verbs. [40] Simply put the main verb in the present tense.

CHAPTER

18

WHAT IS A PARTICIPLE?

A **PARTICIPLE** is a form of a verb that is used primarily in one of two ways: with an auxiliary verb to indicate certain tenses or as an adjective to describe something.

He *has closed* the door.

auxiliary + participle → past tense

He heard me through the *closed* door.

participle describing *door* → adjective

There are two types of participles: the present participle and the past participle.

PRESENT PARTICIPLE

IN ENGLISH

The present participle is easy to recognize because it is the *-ing* form of the verb: *working, studying, dancing, playing.*

The present participle is used primarily as the main verb in compound tenses with the auxiliary verb *to be* (see *What is an Auxiliary Verb?*, p. 46).

She *is writing* with her new pen.

present progressive of *to write*

They *were sleeping.*

past progressive of *to sleep*

IN FRENCH

The present participle, "LE PARTICIPE PRÉSENT," is formed by adding **-ant** to the stem of the **nous** form of the present tense: chant~~ons~~ → chant**ant** *(singing)*, finiss-~~ons~~ → finiss**ant** *(finishing)*.

The present participle is used differently and less frequently in French than in English. Refer to your textbook.

CAREFUL — Remember that the French equivalent of the English tenses formed with an auxiliary + present participle (*she is singing, they were dancing*) do not use participles in French. These English constructions correspond to a simple tense of the French verb.

She is singing.   →   Elle **chante.**

present progressive   present (see p. 58)

They were dancing. → Ils **dansaient.**

past progressive   imperfect (see p. 66)

He will be staying here. → Il **restera** ici.

future progressive   future (see p. 72)

PAST PARTICIPLE

IN ENGLISH

The past participle is formed in several ways. It is the form of the verb that follows *I have: I have* **spoken,** *I have* **written,** *I have* **walked.**

The past participle has two primary uses:

1. as the main verb in compound tenses with the auxiliary verb *to have*

   I *have* **written** all that I have to say.
   He *hasn't* **spoken** to me since our quarrel.

2. as an adjective

   Is the *written* word more important than the *spoken* word?

   describes the noun *word*   describes the noun *word*

IN FRENCH

The past participle, "LE PARTICIPE PASSÉ," can be regular or irregular. Here are the endings of regular verbs:

- **-er** verbs add **-é** to the stem (see p. 42)
- **-ir** verbs add **-i** to the stem
- **-re** verbs add **-u** to the stem

INFINITIVE	STEM	PAST PARTICIPLE
chanter	chant-	chanté
finir	fin-	fini
répondre	répond-	répondu

You will have to memorize irregular past participles individually. As you can see in the examples below, they can be very different from the infinitive.

INFINITIVE	PAST PARTICIPLE
être	été
avoir	eu
lire	lu
comprendre	compris
écrire	écrit

As in English, the past participle can be used as the main verb of a compound tense or as an adjective.

1. as the main verb in compound tenses with the auxiliary **avoir** *(to have)* or **être** *(to be)*

   Nous avons **compris** la leçon.
   *We have **understood** the lesson.*

   Roger est **allé** à la maison.
   *Roger has **gone** home.*

   Many tenses are formed with the auxiliary verbs **avoir** or **être** + the past participle of the main verb. These tenses are discussed in various chapters of this handbook (see *What is the Past Tense?*, p. 63; *What is the Past Perfect Tense?*, p. 69; *What is the Future Perfect Tense?*, p. 75, and pp. 82-3 in *What is the Conditional?*).

2. as an adjective that agrees with the noun it modifies in gender and number (see *What is a Descriptive Adjective?*, p. 88)

   la langue **parlée**
   noun   adjective
   fem. sing. fem. sing. → **parlé** + e
   *the **spoken** language*

   les mots **écrits**
   noun   adjective
   masc. pl. masc. pl. → **écrit** + s
   *the **written** words*

   les lettres **écrites**
   noun   adjective
   fem. pl. fem. pl. → **écrit** + es
   *the **written** letters*

WHAT IS THE PAST TENSE?

The PAST TENSE is used to indicate that an action took place in the past. [1]

> I *saw* you yesterday.

IN ENGLISH

There are several verb forms that indicate that the action took place in the past.[1]

I worked	SIMPLE PAST
I have worked	PRESENT PERFECT
I was working	PAST PROGRESSIVE
I used to work	WITH HELPING VERB USED TO [10]
I did work	PAST EMPHATIC

The simple past is called "simple" because it is a simple tense; that is, it consists of one word (*worked* in the example above). The other past tenses are compound tenses; that is, they consist of more than one word, an auxiliary + a main verb (*was working, did work*). See p. 55 in *What is Meant by Tense?*.

IN FRENCH

There are two French tenses that correspond to all the English past verbal forms listed above: "LE PASSÉ COMPOSÉ" and [20] "L'IMPARFAIT." We'll refer to these two tenses by their French names because their usage does not correspond to a specific English tense.

LE PASSÉ COMPOSÉ (PRESENT PERFECT)

The **passé composé** is formed with the auxiliary verb **avoir** *(to have)* or **être** *(to be)* conjugated in the present tense + the past participle of the main verb (see *What is an Auxiliary Verb?*, p. 46, and pp. 61-2 in *What is a Participle?*).

j'**ai parlé**	*I spoke, I have spoken, I did speak*	[30]
nous **avons parlé**	*we spoke, we have spoken, we did speak*	

    avoir   past participle **parler** *(to speak)*

je **suis allé**	*I went, I have gone, I did go*
il **est allé**	*he went, he has gone, he did go*

    être past participle **aller** *(to go)*

---

[1]A separate section is devoted to the past perfect *(I had worked)*, see p. 69.

SELECTION OF THE AUXILIARY "AVOIR" OR "ÊTRE"

Most verbs use the auxiliary **avoir**. Therefore, it is easier for you to memorize the list of verbs conjugated with **être** and assume that the other verbs are conjugated with **avoir**.

There are approximately sixteen common verbs, sometimes referred to by grammar books as "verbs of motion," that are conjugated with **être**. "Verbs of motion" is not an accurate description of these verbs since some of them, such as **rester** *(to stay, to remain)*, do not imply motion, and some "verbs of motion," such as **courir** *(to run)*, are conjugated with **avoir**. You will find common "**être** verbs" easy to memorize in pairs of opposites:

aller	*to go*	≠	venir	*to come*
retourner	*to return*	≠	rester	*to remain*
entrer	*to come in*	≠	sortir	*to go out*
arriver	*to arrive*	≠	partir	*to leave*
monter	*to climb*	≠	descendre	*to go down*
		≠	tomber	*to fall*
naître	*to be born*	≠	mourir	*to die*

Verbs derived from the above verbs are also conjugated with **être**: **rentrer** *(to return)*, **revenir** *(to come back)*, and **devenir** *(to become)*, among others.

AGREEMENT OF THE PAST PARTICIPLE

The rules of agreement of the past participle depend on whether the auxiliary verb is **avoir** or **être**.

Être — When the auxiliary verb is **être**, the past participle agrees in gender and number with the subject (review the section *What is a Subject?*, p. 29, and p. 37, lines 175-9).

Max **est allé** au cinéma.
subject   past participle
masc. sing. masc. sing. → **allé**
Max went to the movies.

Marie **est allée** au cinéma.
subject   past participle
fem. sing.   fem. sing. → **allé + e**
Mary went to the movies.

Max et Marie **sont allés** au cinéma.
masc. + fem.→ **ils**   past participle
                masc. pl.→ **allé + s** (see p. 37)
Max and Mary went to the movies.

Avoir — When the auxiliary verb is **avoir,** the past participle agrees in gender and number with the direct object of the verb, provided that the direct object comes before (not after) the verb (review the section on direct objects, p. 111, and direct object pronouns, p. 116). ⁸⁰

- direct object pronouns always come before the verb → past participle agrees with the antecedent of the pronoun (p. 31)

Roger veut cette chemise. Il l'a **achetée.**

antecedent	pronoun (**la**)	past participle + **e**
fem. sing.	dir. obj.	fem. sing. → **acheté + e**
	fem. sing.	

*Roger wants this shirt. He **bought** it.*

Roger veut ces livres. Il **les** a **achetés.** ⁹⁰

antecedent	pronoun	past participle + **s**
masc. pl.	dir. obj.	masc. pl. → **acheté + s**
	masc. pl.	

*Roger wants these books. He **bought them.***

Roger veut ces chemises. Il **les** a **achetées.**

antecedent	pronoun	past participle
fem. pl.	dir. obj.	fem. pl. → **acheté + es**
	fem. pl.	

*Roger wants these shirts. He **bought them.***

- direct object nouns can come before the verb → past participle agrees with the noun(s) ¹⁰⁰

Voici la **chemise** que Roger a **achetée.**

| noun dir. obj. | past participle + **e** |
| fem. sing. | fem. sing. → **acheté + e** |

*Here is the **shirt** that Roger **bought.***

Le **fauteuil** et la **chaise** qu'il a **achetés** sont confortables.

noun	noun	past participle
masc. sing.	fem. sing.	masc. pl. → **acheté + s**
direct objects → masc. pl. (see p. 37)		

***The armchair and the chair** that he **bought** are comfortable.*

- direct object nouns can come after the verb → no agreement, the past participle remains in the masculine singular ¹¹⁰

Roger a **acheté** ces chemises.

| past participle | dir. object after the verb |
| masc. sing. | fem. pl. |

*Roger **bought** these shirts.*

Remember the following when using the **passé composé:**
1. Determine whether the verb takes **avoir** or **être** as the auxiliary.
2. Depending on which auxiliary verb is required, apply the ¹²⁰ appropriate rules of agreement.

L'IMPARFAIT (IMPERFECT)

The **imparfait** is a simple tense formed with the stem of the 1st person plural of the present tense of regular and irregular verbs + a set of endings **-ais, -ais, -ait, -ions, -iez, -aient**: nous aim~~ons~~ → j'aim**ais** *(I loved)*; nous pren~~ons~~ → il pren**ait** *(he took)*; nous finiss~~ons~~ → ils finiss**aient** *(they finished)*.

Two English verb forms indicate that the **imparfait** should be used in French:

1. the verb form includes, or could include, *used to, would*

130

    *As a child, I **used to go** to France every year.*
    *As a child, I **would go** to France every year.*
    Comme enfant, j'**allais** en France chaque année.
          imparfait

2. the verb form is in the past progressive tense (see p. 63)

    *At 10:00 P.M. last night I **was sleeping**.*
          past progressive
    A dix heures hier soir je **dormais**.
          imparfait

140

Except for these two English verb forms, the English verb does not indicate whether you should use the **imparfait** or the **passé composé**.

SELECTION: "LE PASSÉ COMPOSÉ" **OR** "L'IMPARFAIT"

Whether to put a verb in the **passé composé** or the **imparfait** often depends on the context. Here are a few guidelines.

▪ when the English verb can't include *used to, would* (see 1 above) put the French verb in the **passé composé**

    *What exercise **did** you **do** last week?*

150

    *I **went** to the pool three times last week.*
      Did do, went cannot be replaced by used to do, used to go.
    Quel exercice **as**-tu **fait** la semaine dernière?
    Je **suis allé** trois fois à la piscine la semaine dernière.
    passé composé

Compare to:

    *What exercise **did** you **do** when you were young?*
    *I **went** to the pool three times a week.*
      Did do, went can be replaced by used to do, used to go.
    Quel exercice **faisais**-tu quand tu **étais** jeune?

160

    J'**allais** à la piscine trois fois par semaine.
    imparfait

- when there is more than one action taking place at the same time in the past and you want to indicate what was going on → **imparfait** when something happened → **passé composé**

> *I **was reading** when he **arrived.***
>> The actions "reading" and "arrived" took place at the same time in the past: what was going on? I was reading → **imparfait**; what happened? He arrived → **passé composé**.
>
> Je **lisais** quand il **est arrivé**.
>   imparfait   passé composé   170

Compare to:

> *I **read**, he **arrived**, then we **ate**.*
>> The series of actions "read," "arrived," and "ate" happened one after another in the past → **passé composé**.
>
> J'**ai lu**, il **est arrivé**, ensuite nous **avons mangé**.
>   passé composé

Sometimes both tenses are possible, but usually one of the two is more logical. Consult your textbook for additional guidelines.   180

CAREFUL — English and French use a different tense in sentences with the word *since* or *for* (when *for* refers to a period of time).

In English — The verb preceding *since* or *for* is in a past tense when the action began in the past and is continuing in the present.

> *I've studied* French *since* H.S.
> *I've been studying* French *since* H.S.
>   past tense (still going on in the preseent)

> *I've studied* French *for* ten years.   190
> *I've been studying* French *for* ten years.
>   past tense (still going on in the present)

In French — The verb preceding **depuis** (*since* or *for*) is in the present tense when the action began in the past and is continuing in the present.

> J'**étudie** le francais **depuis** l'école secondaire.
>   present   since
> *I've studied French since H.S.*
> *I've been studying French since H.S.*

>   200
> J'**étudie** le francais **depuis** dix ans.
>   present   for
> *I've studied French for ten years.*
> *I've been studying French for ten years.*

Pattern (see *Tips for Learning Word Forms*, p. 4)

1. Auxiliary Verb (**avoir** or **être**)

   ▪ Some students find it helpful to pair the verbs that take **être** with their opposites so as to remember them more easily (see p. 64).

   ▪ You might also find it helpful to remember that the first letters of the verbs that take **être** spell "Dr. Mrs. Vandertramp."

   > Descendre Rester (Dr)　　　　Monter Retourner Sortir (Mrs)
   > Venir Aller Naître Devenir Entrer Revenir Tomber Rentrer Arriver Mourir Partir (Vandertramp)

2. Main Verb (past participle)

   ▪ Regular past participle: (see p. 61).

   ▪ Irregular past participle: To be learned as vocabulary.

Practice

1. Sort out the verb cards that take **être** as the auxiliary verb.

   ▪ Look at the French side and write or say sentences, putting the verb in the **passé composé**.

   ▪ Look at the English side and repeat the same exercise as above.

2. Sort out the verb cards that take **avoir** as the auxiliary verb. Repeat the two steps under 1 above.

3. Once you've mastered separately the verbs that take **être** as an auxiliary and those that take **avoir**, mix the two piles.

4. Look at the English side and write or say French sentences putting the verb in the **passé composé**. This time you'll have to remember the auxiliary verb and the past participle.

Flashcards

Add to each of your verb flashcards the **je** form of the **passé composé**. This will show you whether the verb is conjugated with **avoir** or **être** and will give you the past participle form of the main verb.

> prendre　　　　　　　　*to take*
> j'ai pris　　　　　　　　 *I took*

WHAT IS THE PAST PERFECT TENSE?

The **PAST PERFECT TENSE**, also called the **PLUPERFECT**, is used to express an action completed in the past before another action or event that also occurred in the past.[1]

> She suddenly *remembered* that she *had forgotten* her keys.
> |_____| |_____|
>   simple past   past perfect
>   1   2
>
> Both actions 1 and 2 occurred in the past, but action 2
> preceded action 1. Therefore, action 2 is in the past perfect.

IN ENGLISH

The past perfect is formed with the auxiliary ***had*** + the past participle of the main verb: *I had walked, he had seen,* etc. In conversation *had* is often shortened to *'d* (see *What is an Auxiliary Verb?*, p. 46 and pp. 61-2 in *What is a Participle?*).

Don't forget that verb tenses indicate the time that an action occurs. Therefore, when verbs in the same sentence are in the same tense, the actions took place at the same time. In order to show that actions took place at different times, different tenses must be used.

Look at the following examples:

> The mother *was crying* because her son *was leaving*.
> |_____| |_____|
> past progressive   past progressive
>   1   1
>
> Action 1 and action 2 took place at the same time.

> The mother *was crying* because her son *had left*.
> |_____| |_____|
> past progressive   past perfect
>   1   2
>
> Action 2 took place before action 1.

IN FRENCH

The past perfect, **"LE PLUS-QUE-PARFAIT,"** is formed with the auxiliary verb **avoir** or **être** in the **imparfait** (p. 66) + the past participle of the main verb: **j'avais marché** *(I had walked)*, **elle était allée** *(she had gone)*.

---

[1]You can compare this tense with the future perfect that is used when two actions will happen at different times in the future and you want to stress which action will precede the other (see *What is the Future Perfect Tense?*, p. 75).

The rules of agreement of the past participle are the same as for the **passé composé** (see pp. 64-5).

A verb is put in the **plus-que-parfait** in order to stress that the action of that verb took place before the action of a verb in either the **passé composé** or the **imparfait**.

Observe the sequence of events expressed by the past tenses in the following time-line:

VERB TENSE:	Past perfect	Simple past Past progressive	Present
	Plus-que-parfait	**Passé composé Imparfait**	**Présent**
	- 2	- 1	0

————————x————————x————————x—

TIME ACTION TAKES PLACE: $0 \rightarrow$ now
                                            $-1 \rightarrow$ before 0
                                            $-2 \rightarrow$ before -1

- same verb tense $\rightarrow$ same moment in time

    *The mother **was crying** because her son **was leaving**.*
    La mère **pleurait** parce que son fils **partait**.
           | |
        imparfait   imparfait
          -1   -1

    Two actions in the **imparfait** (point -1) show that they took place at the same time in the past (before 0).

- different verb tenses $\rightarrow$ different times

    *The mother **was crying** because her son **had left**.*
    La mère **pleurait** parce que son fils **était parti**.
           | |
        imparfait   plus-que-parfait
          -1   -2

    The action in the **plus-que-parfait** (point -2) occurred before the action in the **imparfait** (point -1).

CAREFUL — You cannot always rely on spoken English to determine when to use the past perfect in French. In many cases English usage permits the use of the simple past to describe an action that preceded another, if it is clear which action came first.

    *Julia **forgot** (that) she **saw** that movie.*
           | |
      simple past   simple past

    *Julia **forgot** (that) she **had seen** that movie.*
           | |_____|
      simple past   past perfect

Although the two sentences above mean the same thing, only the sequence of tenses in the second sentence would be correct in French.

80

Julia **a oublié** qu'elle **avait vu** ce film.

passé composé   plus-que-parfait

-1   -2

The action in the **plus-que-parfait** (point -2) stresses that it was completed before the other action (point -1).

WHAT IS THE FUTURE TENSE?

1 The FUTURE TENSE indicates that an action will take place some time in the future.

> I'll *see* you tomorrow.

IN ENGLISH

The future tense is formed with the auxiliary **will** or **shall** + the dictionary form of the main verb. Note that *shall* is used in formal English (and British English), and *will* in everyday language. In conversation, *shall* and *will* are often shortened to *'ll*.

10
> Roger and Alex *will do* their homework tomorrow.
> I'll *leave* tonight.

IN FRENCH

You do not need an auxiliary to show that an action will take place in the future. Future time is indicated by a simple tense formed with a stem, referred to as the FUTURE STEM, + endings: **-ai, -as, -a, -ons, -ez, -ont.**

- Future stem of regular verbs:
  -er verbs → **je** form of the present tense + **-r**
20 -ir verbs → infinitive
  -re verbs → infinitive without final **–e**

INFINITIVE	FUTURE STEM	
appel**er** (j'appelle)	appeller-	*to call*
fin**ir**	finir-	*to finish*
répond**re** (répondre̸)	répondr-	*to answer*

- The future stems of irregular verbs must be learned as vocabulary as they are unpredictable.

INFINITIVE	FUTURE STEM	
aller	ir-	*to go*
30	venir	viendr-	*to come*
avoir	aur-	*to have*
être	ser-	*to be*

Notice that whatever the stem, regular or irregular, the sound of the letter "r" is always heard before the future endings added to the stem.

CAREFUL — While English uses the present tense after expressions such as *as soon as, when,* and *by the time* that introduce an action that will take place in the future, French uses the future tense.

> *As soon as he **returns**, I **will call**.*   40
> present   future
>
> Dès qu'il **reviendra**, je **téléphonerai**.
> future   future
> action to take place in the future ("as soon as he *will come* . . .")
>
> *She **will come** when she **is** ready.*
> future   present
>
> Elle **viendra** quand elle **sera** prête.
> future   future
> action to take place in the future (". . . when she *will be* ready")   50

French is stricter than English in its use of tenses.

THE IMMEDIATE FUTURE
In English and in French an action that will occur some time in the near future can also be expressed without using the future tense itself, but with a construction that implies the future. This construction is called the **IMMEDIATE FUTURE.**

IN ENGLISH
The immediate future is expressed with the verb *to go* in the present progressive tense + the infinitive of the main verb: *I*   60
am going to walk, she is going to see, etc.

> similar meaning
>
> *I am going **to sing**.*   *I will sing.*
> present progressive   future tense
> of *to go* + infinitive   of *to sing*

IN FRENCH
The same construction exists in French. It is called "**LE FUTUR IMMÉDIAT**" or "**LE FUTUR PROCHE**" because the future action is considered nearer at hand than an action expressed by a verb   70
in the future tense.

The immediate future is formed with the verb **aller** *(to go)* in the present tense + the infinitive of the main verb: **je vais marcher** *(I'm going to walk)*, **elle va voir** *(she's going to see)*.

Look at the difference between the forms of the immediate future and the future tense.

80

Je **vais chanter.**	Je **chanterai.**
present of **aller** + infinitive	future tense
immediate future	of **chanter**
I am going to sing.	*I will sing.*
present of *to go* + infinitive	future tense
immediate future	of *to sing*

In spoken French, the immediate future often replaces the future tense.

STUDY TIPS — THE FUTURE TENSE

Pattern (see *Tips for Learning Vocabulary*, p. 2)

1. Future stems (see p. 72)
2. Endings (see your textbook and *Study Tips — Verb conjugations*, p. 43)
   - The 1st, 2nd, and 3rd persons singular, as well as the 3rd person plural, are identical to the same persons of the present tense of the verb **avoir**: –ai, –as, –a, and –ont.
   - The 1st and 2nd persons plural are identical to endings of the same persons of the present tense of most verbs: **–ons** and **–ez.**

Flashcards

On your verb cards add the irregular future stem, if there is one. Note: the future stem will also be the stem for the conditional (see *What is the Conditional?*, p. 81).

     vouloir   to want
     voudr-   *(stem: future/conditional)*

Practice

1. Sort out the verbs with regular future stems.
   - Look at the French side. Write (on a separate sheet of paper) or say sentences putting the verb in the future tense.
   - Look at the English side. Write (on a separate sheet of paper) or say French sentences putting the verb in the future tense.
2. Sort out the verbs with irregular future stems. Repeat the two steps under 1 above.
3. Mix the pile of verbs with regular and irregular future stems. Repeat the two steps under 1 above.

WHAT IS THE FUTURE PERFECT TENSE?

The **FUTURE PERFECT TENSE** is used to express an action that will ₁
occur before another action in the future or before a specific
time in the future.[1]

> By the time we leave, he *will have finished*.
> ⎣__future event__⎦ ⎣__future perfect__⎦
>   2   1

> Both action 1 and 2 will occur at some future time, but action 1
> will be completed before action 2 takes place. Therefore, action 1
> is in the future perfect tense.

> I won't meet him. I *will have left* before he arrives.
>   ⎣__future perfect__⎦ ⎣__future event__⎦   10
>   1   2

> Both action 1 and 2 will occur at some future time, but action 1
> will be completed before action 2 takes place. Therefore, action 1
> is in the future perfect tense.

IN ENGLISH

The future perfect is formed with the auxiliary **will have** +
the past participle of the main verb: *I will have walked, she
will have gone*. In conversation *will* is often shortened
to *'ll* (see *What is an Auxiliary Verb?*, p. 46 and pp. 61-2 in *What
is a Participle?*).

The future perfect is often used following expressions such as   20
by then, by that time, by + a date.

> By the end of the month, he*'ll have graduated*.
> By June, I*'ll have saved* enough to buy a car.

IN FRENCH

The future perfect, **"LE FUTUR ANTÉRIEUR,"** is formed with the
auxiliary **avoir** or **être** in the future tense + the past participle
of the main verb: **j'aurai marché** *(I'll have walked)*, **elle sera
allée** *(she'll have gone)*. See *What is the Future Tense?*, p. 72.

The rules of agreement of the past participle are the same   30
as for the **passé composé** (see pp. 64-5).

As in English, a verb is put in the **futur antérieur** tense in
order to stress that the action of that verb will have taken
place before the action of a verb in the future or before a specific future time.

---

[1]You can compare this tense to the past perfect that is used when two actions occurred at
different times in the past and you want to stress which action preceded the other (see
What is the Past Perfect Tense?, p. 69).

Observe the sequence of events expressed by the future tenses in the following time-line:

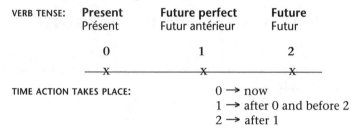

VERB TENSE:	**Present**	**Future perfect**	**Future**
	Présent	Futur antérieur	Futur

0   1   2

TIME ACTION TAKES PLACE: 0 → now
1 → after 0 and before 2
2 → after 1

*When I've **learned** French, I'll go to Paris.*
Quand j'**aurai appris** le français, j'**irai** à Paris.
                        1   2

The action in the **futur antérieur** (point 1) will occur before the action in the **futur** (point 2).

*Before school starts, I'll **have left**.*
Avant la rentrée des classes, je **serai parti**.
                        2   1

The action in the **futur antérieur** (point 1) will occur before the future event (point 2).

CAREFUL — While English uses the present tense after conjunctions such as *when* (**quand**) and *as soon as* (**dès que**), French uses the **futur antérieur**.

*When he **finishes** this course, he'**ll understand** French.*
           present   future
Quand il **aura fini** ce cours, il **comprendra** le français.
       futur antérieur   futur

Consult your textbook for other uses of the **futur antérieur**.

WHAT IS MEANT BY MOOD?

MOOD in the grammatical sense is a term applied to verb tenses. [1]
Different moods serve different purposes. For instance, verb
tenses that state a fact belong to one mood *(you are studying, you
studied)* and the verb tense that gives orders belongs to another
(Study!). Some moods have multiple tenses, others have only one
tense.

You should recognize the names of moods so that you will
know what your French textbook is referring to when it uses
these terms. You will learn when to use the various moods as
you learn verbs and their tenses.

IN ENGLISH [10]

Verbs can be in one of four moods:

1. The **INDICATIVE MOOD** is used to state the action of the verb;
   that is, to *indicate* facts. This is the most common mood
   and most of the verb forms that you use in everyday conversation belong to the indicative mood. The majority of
   the tenses studied in this handbook belong to the indicative mood: for instance, the present tense (see p. 58), the
   past tense (see p. 63), and the future tense (p. 72).

   > Roger *studies* French. [20]
   > present indicative

   > Mary *was* here.
   > past indicative

   > They *will come* tomorrow.
   > future indicative

2. The **IMPERATIVE MOOD** is used to give commands or orders.
   This mood is not divided into tenses (see *What is the Imperative?*, p. 79).

   > Roger, *study* French now! [30]
   > Mary, *be* home on time!

3. The **SUBJUNCTIVE MOOD** is used to express an attitude or
   feeling toward the action of the verb; it is *subjective* about
   it. In English, this mood is not divided into tenses (see
   What is the Subjunctive?, p. 85).

   > The school requires that students *study* French.
   > I wish that Mary *were* here.
   > The teacher recommends that he *do* his homework.

4. The CONDITIONAL MOOD is primarily used to express: 1. a wish or desire more politely, and 2. a hypothetical state of affairs or an event that can only be realized if another event occurs. It has two tenses: the present conditional and the past conditional (see *What is the Conditional?*, p. 81).

> *Would* you *close* the door.
> He *would go* to France if he had the money.
> Mary *would have passed* the test, if she had studied.

IN FRENCH

Verbs can be in one of four moods:

1. As in English, the INDICATIVE MOOD is the most common and most of the tenses you will learn belong to this mood.

2. As in English, the IMPERATIVE MOOD is used to give orders. It is not divided into tenses.

3. Unlike in English, however, the SUBJUNCTIVE MOOD is used very frequently. It has two main tenses: the present subjunctive and the past subjunctive. The term "present subjunctive" is used to distinguish it from the "present indicative" and the "present conditional."

4. As in English, the CONDITIONAL MOOD has two tenses: the present conditional and the past conditional. The term "present conditional" is used to distinguish it from the "present indicative" and the "present subjunctive."

When there is no reference to mood, the tense belongs to the most common mood, the indicative.

WHAT IS THE IMPERATIVE?

The **IMPERATIVE** is a verbal mood used to give someone an order. [1]
The **AFFIRMATIVE IMPERATIVE** is an order to do something. The **NEGATIVE IMPERATIVE** is an order not to do something (see *What is Meant by Mood?*, p. 77).

> *Come* here!
> *Don't come* here!

IN ENGLISH

There are two types of command, depending on who is told to do, or not to do, something.

1. **"You" COMMAND** — When an order is given to one or more [10]
persons, the dictionary form of the verb is used.

AFFIRMATIVE IMPERATIVE	NEGATIVE IMPERATIVE
Answer the phone.	*Don't answer* the phone.
Clean your room.	*Don't clean* your room.
Speak softly.	*Don't speak* softly.

2. **"We" COMMAND** — When an order is given to oneself as well as to others, the phrase *let us* is used + the dictionary form of the verb. *Let us* is often contracted to *let's*, with the letter "u" replaced by an apostrophe.

AFFIRMATIVE IMPERATIVE	NEGATIVE IMPERATIVE	[20]
Let's leave.	*Let's not leave.*	
Let's go to the movies.	*Let's not go* to the movies.	

IN FRENCH

As in English, there are affirmative and negative commands. To form the imperative, most verbs use the present tense, dropping the subject pronoun. Your textbook will go over the verbs that have an irregular imperative.

1. **"TU" COMMAND** — When an order is given to a person to whom one says **tu**, the **tu**-form of the present tense is used. [30]

AFFIRMATIVE IMPERATIVE	NEGATIVE IMPERATIVE
Viens.	**Ne viens pas.**
Come.	*Don't come.*
Prends le livre.	**Ne prends pas** le livre.
Take the book.	*Don't take the book.*

Note that in the imperative -**er** verbs drop the final "-s" in the **tu**-form:

PRESENT TENSE	IMPERATIVE
tu manges	**Mange!**
you eat	*Eat!*
tu ne chantes **pas**	Ne **chante** pas!
you don't sing	*Don't sing!*

2. "**Vous**" COMMAND — When an order is given to a person to whom one says **vous**, or to more than one person, the **vous**-form of the present tense is used.

AFFIRMATIVE IMPERATIVE	NEGATIVE IMPERATIVE
Venez.	**Ne venez pas.**
Come.	*Don't come.*
Prenez le livre.	**Ne prenez pas** le livre.
Take the book.	*Don't take the book.*

3. "**Nous**" COMMAND — When an order is given to oneself as well as to others, the **nous**-form of the present tense is used.

AFFIRMATIVE IMPERATIVE	NEGATIVE IMPERATIVE
Allons.	**N'allons pas.**
Let's go.	*Let's not go.*
Prenons le livre.	**Ne prenons pas** le livre.
Let's take the book.	*Let's not take the book.*

In English and in French the absence of the subject pronoun in the sentence is a good indication that you are dealing with an imperative and not a present tense (see *What is the Present Tense?*, p. 58).

Vous répondez au téléphone.
You answer the phone.
present

Répondez au téléphone.
Answer the phone.
imperative

CAREFUL — French verbs in the affirmative imperative tense take a special set of object pronouns (see p. 126 in *What is a Disjunctive Pronoun?*).

WHAT IS THE CONDITIONAL?

The **CONDITIONAL** is a verbal mood that gets its name because its
tenses are primarily used in sentences that state a condition (see
What is Meant by Mood?, p. 77).

> If I were offered the job, I *would take* it.
>   <u>condition</u>   <u>verb in the conditional</u>

These hypothetical statements are made up of two clauses (see
p. 106).

- the *IF*-CLAUSE — the clause starting with "if" stating a condition → the verb is in the indicative mood, except for the
  verb *to be* that goes in the subjunctive mood
- the **RESULT CLAUSE** — the clause stating what would occur if
  the condition were fulfilled → the verb is in the conditional mood

The conditional mood has two tenses: a present and a past
tense.

PRESENT CONDITIONAL IN IF-CLAUSES
IN ENGLISH

The present conditional is formed with the auxiliary **would** +
the dictionary form of the main verb: *I would eat, they would
talk, we would go.* (See *What is an Auxiliary Verb?*, p. 46.)

The present conditional is used in the following ways:

1. in polite requests

    > *Would* you please *close* the door.

2. in the result clause of a hypothetical or contrary-to-fact
   statement

   When the condition refers to the present time, the verb of
   the result clause is in the present conditional and the verb
   of the *if*-clause is in the simple past tense or, for the verb
   to be, in the subjunctive *(were)*, regardless which clause
   comes first in the sentence.

   > Paul *would buy* a car, if he had money.
   >   subject verb   subject verb
   >   present condition   simple past

   > Hypothetical: Paul does not have the money now, if he did he
   > would buy a car. Possibility of his having money in the future
   > and buying a car.

1

10

20

30

If Paul *were* in Paris, he *would join* us.

subject　verb *to be*　　subject　verb
　　　　subjunctive　　　　　present conditional

Contrary-to-fact: Paul is not in Paris now and can't join us.

IN FRENCH

Unlike in English, you do not need an auxiliary to form the present conditional, "LE CONDITIONNEL PRÉSENT." It is a simple tense formed with the future stem (see p. 72) + the imperfect endings (p. 66): je **parler- + ais**, il **ir- + ait**, nous **vendr- + ions** (*I would speak, he would go, we would sell*).

As in English, the present conditional is used in two ways:

1. in polite requests

Pourriez-vous fermer la porte?
present conditional
Would you **please** *close the door?*

2. in the result clause of a hypothetical or contrary-to-fact statement

When the condition refers to the present time, the verb of the result clause is in the present conditional and the verb of the **si** *(if)*-clause is in the **imparfait**, regardless which clause comes first in the sentence.

Paul **achèterait** une voiture, s'il **avait** l'argent,
present conditional　　　　　**imparfait**
Paul **would buy** *a car, if he* **had** *the money.*

CAREFUL — The auxiliary *would* does not correspond to the French conditional when it stands for *used to*, as in "she *would talk* while he painted." In this sentence, it means *used to talk* and requires the imperfect (see p. 66).

PAST CONDITIONAL IN IF-CLAUSES

IN ENGLISH

The past conditional is formed with the auxiliaries **would have** + the past participle of the main verb (see p. 61): *I would have eaten, they would have talked, we would have gone.* In spoken English *would have* is often shortened to *would've.*

When the condition refers to the past, the verb of the result clause is in the past conditional and the verb of the *if*-clause is in the past perfect tense, regardless which clause comes first in the sentence.

If Paul *had had* money, he *would have bought* a car.
　　past perfect　　　　　　past conditional

A fact: Paul did not have the money, therefore he did not buy a car.

IN FRENCH

The past conditional, "LE CONDITIONNEL PASSÉ," is formed with
the auxiliary **avoir** or **être** in the present conditional + the
past participle of the main verb: j'**aurais parlé**, il **serait allée**,
nous **aurions vendu** *(I would have spoken, he would have gone,
we would have sold)*. The same rules of agreement apply as for
the **passé composé**, see pp. 64-5.

As in English, when the condition refers to time in the
past, the verb of the result clause is in the past conditional
and the verb of the **si** *(if)*-clause is in the **plus-que-parfait**,
regardless which clause comes first in the sentence (see *What
is the Past Perfect Tense?*, p. 69).

Paul **aurait acheté** une voiture, s'il **avait eu** l'argent, .
     past conditional   plus-que-parfait
*If Paul **had had** the money, he **would have bought** a car.*

Si Paul **avait eu** l'argent, il l'**aurait achetée**.
   plus-que-parfait   direct object   past participle **acheté + e**
                   fem. sing.   referring to **la voiture** (fem. sing.)
*If Paul **had had** the money, he **would have bought** it.*

SUMMARY: *IF*-CLAUSES SEQUENCE OF TENSES

In English and in French the *if*-clause can come before or after
the result clause and the tense of one clause depends on the
tense of the other.

■ The condition is possible; if met, the result will take place now
or in the future.

IF-CLAUSE ◄————————►	RESULT CLAUSE
present	future
présent	**futur**

*If he **studies**, he **will pass**.*
    present   future

S'il **étudie**, il **réussira**.
    présent   conditionnel présent

■ The condition is unlikely; if met, the result will take place in
the future.

IF-CLAUSE ◄————————►	RESULT CLAUSE
simple past	present conditional
imparfait	**conditionnel présent**

*If he **studied**, he **would pass**.*
    simple past   present conditional

S'il **étudiait**, il **réussirait**.
   imparfait   conditionnel présent

■ The condition wasn't met in the past; but if it had been, the result would have occurred.

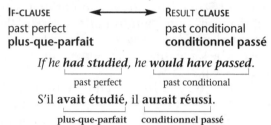

IF-CLAUSE	←——————→	RESULT CLAUSE
past perfect		past conditional
plus-que-parfait		**conditionnel passé**

If he ***had studied****, he* ***would have passed****.*
   past perfect   past conditional

S'il **avait étudié**, il **aurait réussi**.
  plus-que-parfait conditionnel passé

USE OF THE CONDITIONAL IN INDIRECT SPEECH

DIRECT SPEECH is a word-for-word quotation of what someone said as opposed to INDIRECT SPEECH that repeats or reports someone's words. In written form a direct statement is always between quotation marks.

In both English and French the conditional is used in the reported statement.

IN ENGLISH

Here is an example of a direct statement changed to an indirect statement.

DIRECT STATEMENT Paul said: *"Mary will arrive this evening."*
         1   2
         past   future

INDIRECT STATEMENT Paul said *Mary would arrive this evening.*
         1   2
         past present conditional

In the direct statement, action 2 is a quotation in the future tense. In the indirect statement, action 2 is called a FUTURE-IN-THE-PAST because it takes place after another action in the past, "Paul said."

IN FRENCH

As in English, the conditional is used in an indirect statement to express a future-in-the-past.

DIRECT STATEMENT Paul a dit: "Marie **viendra** ce soir."
         1   2
       passé composé futur

INDIRECT STATEMENT Paul a dit que Marie **viendrait** ce soir.
         1   2
      passé composé conditionnel présent

26

WHAT IS THE SUBJUNCTIVE?

The **SUBJUNCTIVE** is a verbal mood used to express a wish, emo- ₁
tions, uncertainty, demands, or other similar attitude toward a
fact or an idea (see *What is Meant by Mood?*, p. 77).

> I wish he *were* here.
>
> subject's   subjunctive
> wish

> The teacher insisted that the homework *be* neat.
>
>   subject's   subjunctive
>   demand

IN ENGLISH 10

The subjunctive verb forms are difficult to recognize because
they are spelled like other tenses of the verb: the dictionary
form and the simple past tense.

INDICATIVE	SUBJUNCTIVE
He *writes* a lot.	The course requires that he *write* a lot.
indicative present *to write*	subjunctive (same as dictionary form)
I *am* in Paris.	I wish I *were* in Paris.
indicative present *to be*	subjunctive (same as past tense)

The subjunctive is used in very few constructions. In spoken ²⁰
English, it is primarily used following expressions such as *to
require, demand,* and *to wish.* Unfortunately English usage will
rarely indicate when to use it in French.

IN FRENCH

Unlike in English, the subjunctive mood is used very frequently. There are various tenses, but the present and the
past subjunctive are the most common.

The subjunctive mood is used primarily in dependent
clauses following certain verbs, expressions, and conjunc- ₃₀
tions when the subjects of the main and dependent clauses
are different. Be sure to memorize the verbs, expressions, and
conjunctions that trigger the subjunctive in dependent
clauses and to consult your textbook for the verb form used
when they are not followed by a dependent clause.

Here are a few examples. The dependent clause starting
with **que** *(that)* is underlined.

- verbs of will or desire

Je veux que tu ailles à l'école.

vouloir	aller
subject **je**	subject **tu**
indicative	subjunctive

I want you to go to school.
(word-for-word: "*I want that you go to school*")

Elle préfère que je lise le livre en français.

préférer	lire
subject **elle**	subject **je**
indicative	subjunctive

She prefers that I read the book in French.

- expressions of necessity

Il faut que j'apprenne le français.

falloir	apprendre
subject **il**	subject **je**
indicative	subjunctive

It is necessary that I learn French.

- verbs of doubt

Je doute que Jade sache parler français.

douter	savoir
subject **je**	subject **Jade**
indicative	subjunctive

I doubt (that) Jade knows how to speak French.

- expressions of emotion

Les enfants sont heureux que vous veniez ce soir.

être	venir
subject **les enfants**	subject **vous**
indicative	subjunctive

The children are happy (that) you are coming this evening.

- expressions of opinion

Il est dommage qu'elle soit malade.

regretter	être
subject **il**	subject **elle**
indicative	subjunctive

It is too bad (that) she is sick.

Since English structures are not relevant, we refer you to your textbook regarding the use of the subjunctive in French.

STUDY TIPS — SUBJUNCTIVE

When memorizing the forms of the present subjunctive compare them to the forms of the present indicative. It will help you remember what distinguishes one from the other.

WHAT IS AN ADJECTIVE?

An **ADJECTIVE** is a word that describes a noun or a pronoun. [1]
There are different types of adjectives that are classified
according to the way they describe a noun or pronoun.

DESCRIPTIVE ADJECTIVE — A descriptive adjective indicates a
quality; it tells what kind of noun it is (see p. 88).

> She read an *interesting* book.
> He has *brown* eyes.

POSSESSIVE ADJECTIVE — A possessive adjective shows possession;
it tells whose noun it is (see p. 94).

> *His* book is lost. [10]
> *Our* parents are away.

INTERROGATIVE ADJECTIVE — An interrogative adjective asks a question about a noun (see p. 99).

> *What* book is lost?
> *Which* parents did you speak to?

DEMONSTRATIVE ADJECTIVE — A demonstrative adjective points out
a noun (see p. 101).

> *This* teacher is excellent.
> *That* question is very appropriate. [20]

IN ENGLISH

English adjectives usually do not change their form, regardless of the noun or pronoun described.

IN FRENCH

The principal difference between English and French adjectives is that while in English adjectives do not change their
form, in French adjectives change in order to agree in gender
and number with the noun or pronoun they modify.

STUDY TIPS — DESCRIPTIVE ADJECTIVES (SEE P. 90)

STUDY TIPS — POSSESSIVE ADJECTIVES (SEE P. 97)

CHAPTER

28

WHAT IS A DESCRIPTIVE ADJECTIVE?

1   A DESCRIPTIVE ADJECTIVE is a word that indicates a quality of a
noun or pronoun. As the name implies, it *describes* the noun or
pronoun.

> The book is *interesting.*
> noun   descriptive
> described   adjective

IN ENGLISH

A descriptive adjective does not change form, regardless of
the noun or pronoun it modifies.

10
> The students are *intelligent.*
> She is an *intelligent* person.
>
> > The adjective *intelligent* is the same although the persons
> > described are different in number *(students* is plural and
> > *person* is singular).

IN FRENCH

While English descriptive adjectives never change form,
French descriptive adjectives change form in order to agree
in gender and number with the noun or pronoun they
modify.

20
Most regular adjectives add an "-e" to the masculine form
to make the feminine form and an "-s" to the masculine singular or the feminine singular form to make it plural.

> *The book is **blue.***   Le livre est **bleu.**
>   masc.   masc.
>   sing.   sing.
>
> *The dress is **blue.***   La robe est **bleue.**
>   fem.   fem. (**bleu + e**)
>   sing.   sing.

30
> *The books are **blue.***   Les livres sont **bleus.**
>   masc.   masc. (**bleu + s**)
>   pl.   pl.
>
> *The dresses are **blue.***   Les robes sont **bleues.**
>   fem.   fem. (**bleu + es**)
>   pl.   pl.

When you learn a new adjective, make sure you learn how to
make its feminine and plural forms.

ATTRIBUTIVE AND PREDICATE ADJECTIVES

IN ENGLISH

Descriptive adjectives are divided into two groups depending on how they are connected to the noun they modify.

1. A **PREDICATE ADJECTIVE** is connected to the noun it modifies, always the subject of the sentence, by a **LINKING VERB** such as *to be, to feel, to look.*

> The children are *good.*
> noun   linking   predicate
> described verb   adjective

> The house looks *small.*
> noun   linking   predicate
> described verb   adjective

2. An **ATTRIBUTIVE ADJECTIVE** is connected directly to the noun it modifies and always precedes it.

> The *good* children were praised.
> attributive noun
> adjective   described

> The family lives in a *small* house.
> attributive noun
> adjective   described

IN FRENCH

As in English, descriptive adjectives can be identified as predicate or attributive adjectives, depending on how they are connected to the noun they modify. As in English, French predicate adjectives are placed after a linking verb such as **être** *(to be)* and follow the same word order.

While English attributive descriptive adjectives always come before the noun they modify, most, but not all, French attributive descriptive adjectives come after the noun they modify.

> Elle lit un **livre intéressant**.
> *She is reading an **interesting book.***

However, some common French descriptive adjectives, come before the noun they modify.

> Daniel est un **beau garçon** et Julia est une **jolie fille**.
> *Daniel is a **handsome boy** and Julia is a **pretty girl.***

Your textbook will tell you, and you will have to learn, which French descriptive adjectives precede and which follow the noun they modify.

Flashcards (see *Tips for Learning Vocabulary*, p. 2)

1. Create flashcards indicating the adjective twice on the French side, once modifying a masculine noun and once modifying a feminine noun. This will show you the masculine and feminine forms of the adjective and whether it is placed before or after the noun it modifies. (Refer to your textbook for the placement of adjectives in a sentence.)

un stylo vert	*a green pen*
une robe verte	*a green dress*
un vieux livre	*an old book*
une vieille robe	*an old dress*

2. If the adjective has irregular singular or plural forms, illustrate them.

le beau jardin	*the beautiful garden*
les beaux jardins	*the beautiful gardens*
le bel appartement	*the beautiful apartment*
les beaux appartements	*the beautiful apartments*
la belle maison	*the beautiful house*

Practice

Write short sentences using the descriptive adjectives you learned, concentrating on the descriptive adjectives with irregular forms.

WHAT IS MEANT BY COMPARISON
OF ADJECTIVES?

The term **COMPARISON OF ADJECTIVES** is used when two or more   1
persons or things have the same quality indicated by a descriptive adjective and we want to show which of these persons or
things has a greater, lesser, or equal degree of that quality.

comparison of adjectives

Paul is *tall* but Mary is *taller*.

adjective   adjective
modifies *Paul*   modifies *Mary*

Mary has a greater degree of that quality (i.e., she is *taller* than Paul).

In English and in French there are two types of comparison: 10
comparative and superlative.

COMPARATIVE

The comparison can indicate that one or the other person or
thing has more, less, or the same amount of that quality.

IN ENGLISH

Let's go over the three degrees of comparison:

1. The comparison of **GREATEST DEGREE** (more) is formed differently depending on the length of the adjective being com-
   pared.   20

   ▪ short adjective + *-er* + *than*

     Roger is tall*er than* Julia.
     She is smart*er than* her sister.

   ▪ *more* + longer adjective + *than*

     Roger is *more* intelligent *than* his brother.
     His car is *more* expensive *than* ours.

2. The comparison of **LESSER DEGREE** (less) is formed as follows:
   not as + adjective + *as,* or *less* + adjective + *than.*   30

     Julia is *not as* tall *as* Roger.
     My car is *less* expensive *than* your car.

3. The comparison of **EQUAL DEGREE** (same) is formed as follows: *as* + adjective + *as.*

     Daniel is *as* tall *as* Jade.
     My car is *as* expensive *as* yours.

IN FRENCH

There are the same three degrees of comparison of adjectives as in English.

Like all French adjectives, French comparative adjectives agree with the noun they modify, in this case the subject of the sentence.

1. The comparison of GREATER DEGREE is formed as follows: **plus** *(more)* + adjective + **que** *(than)*.

> Daniel est **plus** actif **que** Jade.
>
> masc. sing. agrees with subject → Daniel (masc. sing.)
>
> *Daniel is **more** active **than** Jade.*

2. The comparison of LESSER DEGREE is formed as follows: **moins** *(less)* + adjective + **que** *(than)*.

> Jade est **moins** active **que** Daniel.
>
> fem. sing. agrees with subject → Jade (fem. sing.)
>
> *Jade is **less** active **than** Daniel.*

3. The comparison of EQUAL DEGREE is formed as follows: **aussi** *(as)* + adjective + **que** *(as)*.

> Les filles sont **aussi** actives **que** les garçons.
>
> fem. pl. agrees with subject → les filles (fem. pl.)
>
> *The girls are **as** active **as** the boys.*

SUPERLATIVE

The superlative is used to stress the highest and lowest degrees of a quality.

IN ENGLISH

Let's go over the two degrees of the superlative:

1. The superlative of GREATEST DEGREE is formed differently depending on the length of the adjective.

   ▪ ***the*** + short adjective + ***-est***

   > Jade is *the* smart*est*.
   > My car is *the* cheap*est*.

   ▪ ***the most*** + long adjective

   > Daniel is *the most* intelligent.
   > His car is *the most* expensive.

2. The superlative of LOWEST DEGREE is formed as follows: ***the least*** + adjective.

   > Daniel is *the least* active.
   > His car is *the least* expensive.

IN FRENCH ₈₀

As in English, there are two degrees of the superlative.

1. The superlative of GREATEST DEGREE is formed as follows: **le, la,** or **les** (depending on the gender and number of the noun described) + **plus** *(most)* + adjective.

> Jade est **la plus active** de la famille.
> <u>fem. sing.</u>
> *Jade is **the most active** in the family.*

> Daniel est **le plus grand.**
> <u>masc. sing.</u> ₉₀
> *Daniel is **the tallest.***

> <u>Jade et Daniel</u> sont **les plus intelligents** de la classe.
> masc. pl. (see p. 37)
> *Jade and Daniel are **the most intelligent** in the class.*

2. The superlative of LOWEST DEGREE is formed as follows: **le, la,** or **les** (depending on the gender and number of the noun described) + **moins** *(less)* + adjective.

> Alex est **le moins actif** de la classe.
> <u>masc. sing.</u> ₁₀₀
> *Alex is **the least active** in the class.*

CAREFUL — In English and in French a few adjectives have irregular forms of comparison that you will have to memorize.

ADJECTIVE	Cette pomme est **bonne.**
	*This apple is **good.***
COMPARATIVE	Cette pomme est **meilleure.**
	*This apple is **better.***
SUPERLATIVE	Cette pomme est **la meilleure.**
	*This apple is **the best.***

₁₁₀

The English comparative form *better* serves as a comparative adjective and as a comparative adverb. In each case it has a different French equivalent and follows the rules of its own part of speech (see *Adverb or adjective?*, p. 104).

Better comparing nouns = comparative of the adjective *good* **(bon)** → **meilleur** (adjective agrees with the noun it modifies)

> *It is **a good** film. The play is **better.***
> C'est un **bon** film. La pièce est **meilleure.**

Better comparing verbs = comparative of the adverb *well* **(bien)** → **mieux** (adverb does not change form) ₁₂₀

> *Alex sings **well.** Julia sings **better.***
> Alex chante **bien.** Julia chante **mieux.**

CHAPTER

30

WHAT IS A POSSESSIVE ADJECTIVE?

1   A **POSSESSIVE ADJECTIVE** is a word that describes a noun by showing who possesses that noun.

> Whose house is that? It's *my* house.
>
> possessor is *me*   object possessed

IN ENGLISH

Like subject pronouns, possessive adjectives are identified according to the person they represent (see p. 33).

SINGULAR POSSESSOR		
1ˢᵀ PERSON		my
2ᴺᴰ PERSON		your
	MASCULINE	his
3ᴿᴰ PERSON	FEMININE	her
	NEUTER	its
PLURAL POSSESSOR		
1ˢᵀ PERSON		our
2ᴺᴰ PERSON		your
3ᴿᴰ PERSON		their

10

A possessive adjective changes according to the possessor, regardless of the noun possessed.

20

> Is that Daniel's house? Yes, it is *his* house.
> Is that Alice's house? Yes, it is *her* house.
>> Although the object possessed is the same *(house)*, different possessive adjectives *(his* and *her)* are used because the possessors are different *(Daniel* and *Alice)*.
>
> Is that Daniel's house? Yes, it is *his* house.
> Are those Daniel's keys? Yes, they are *his* keys.
>> Although the objects possessed are different *(house* and *keys)*, the same possessive adjective *(his)* is used because the possessor is the same *(Daniel)*.

30

IN FRENCH

Like in English, French possessive adjectives change according to the possessor, but unlike English they also agree, like all French adjectives, in gender and number with the noun possessed.

Let us look at French possessive adjectives to see how they are formed. We have the divided the French possessive adjectives into two groups.

SINGULAR POSSESSOR (1ˢᵀ, 2ᴺᴰ AND 3ᴿᴰ PERS. SING.)
my, your (tu-form), his, her, its   40

In French, each of these possessive adjectives has three forms depending on the gender and number of the noun possessed: the masculine singular, the feminine singular, and the plural (the same for both genders).

To choose the correct possessive adjective:

1. Indicate the possessor with the first letter of the possessive adjective.

my	**m-**
your	**t-** (**tu**-form)
his *her* *its*	**s-**

50

2. Choose the ending according to the gender and number of the noun possessed.

- noun possessed is masculine singular or feminine singular beginning with a vowel → add **-on**

Alice lit **mon** livre.	*Alice reads **my** book.*
masc. sing.	noun possessed
Alice lit **ton** livre.	*Alice reads **your** book.*
Alice lit **son** livre.	*Alice reads **her** (**his**) book.*

60

Max connaît **mon** amie.	*Max knows **my** friend.*
fem. sing. begins with vowel	noun possessed
Max connaît **ton** amie.	*Max knows **your** friend.*
Max connaît **son** amie.	*Max knows **his** (**her**) friend.*

- noun possessed is feminine singular beginning with a consonant → add **-a**

Max lit **ma** lettre.	*Max reads **my** letter.*
fem. sing.	noun possessed
Max lit **ta** lettre.	*Max reads **your** letter.*
Max lit **sa** lettre.	*Max reads **his** (**her**) letter.*

70

- noun possessed is plural → add **-es**

Alice lit **mes** livres.	*Alice reads **my** books.*
masc. pl.	noun possessed
Max lit **tes** lettres.	*Max reads **your** letters.*
fem. pl.	
Elle lit **ses** livres.	*She is reading **his** (**her**) books.*
masc. pl.	

80

3. Select the proper form according to the two steps above.

Let us apply the above steps to examples:

> *Roger is looking at **his** mother.*
> 1. Possessor: *his* → 3rd pers. sing. → **s-**
> 2. Noun possessed: **mère** *(mother)* → feminine singular → **a**
> 3. Selection: **s- + -a**
>
> Roger regarde **sa** mère.

90

> *Roger is looking at **his** father.*
> 1. Possessor: *his* → 3rd pers. sing. → **s-**
> 2. Noun possessed: **père** *(father)* → masculine singular → **on**
> 3. Selection: **s- + -on**
>
> Roger regarde **son** père.

CAREFUL — Make sure that the ending of the possessive adjective agrees with the noun it modifies and not with the possessor. Context usually makes it clear whether you are referring to *his* or *her*.

PLURAL POSSESSOR (1ST, 2ND AND 3RD PERS. PL.)

100   our, your (vous-form), their

In French, each of these possessive adjectives has two forms depending on the number of the noun possessed; that is, whether the noun possessed is singular or plural.

■ noun possessed is singular → **notre**, **votre**, or **leur**

Marie est **notre** fille.	*Mary is **our** daughter.*
⎸ noun possessed singular	
Roger lit **votre** lettre.	*Roger reads **your** letter.*
Ils lisent **leur** lettre.	*They read **their** letter.*

110   ■ noun possessed is plural → **nos**, **vos**, or **leurs**

Les parents sont **nos** amis.	*The parents are **our** friends.*
⎸ noun possessed plural	
Alice lit **vos** livres.	*Alice reads **your** books.*
Elles lisent **leurs** lettres.	*They read **their** letters.*

Although **votre** and **vos** are classified as forms of the second person plural they can refer to a single possessor when used in a formal form of address (see pp. 34-5).

120   **CAREFUL** — Make sure that you use the same "you" form, either familiar or formal, for the verb and the possessive adjective: *"You* are reading *your* letter" would be either "**Tu** lis **ta** lettre" or "**Vous** lisez **votre** lettre."

SUMMARY

Here is a chart you can use as a reference.

POSSESSOR SINGULAR		NOUN POSSESSED	
		SINGULAR	PLURAL
my {	MASC.	mon	
	FEM. + VOWEL	mon	mes
	FEM.	ma	
your (***tu*** form) {	MASC.	ton	
	FEM. + VOWEL	ton	tes
	FEM.	ta	
(***vous*** formal form)		votre	vos
his, her, its {	MASC.	son	
	FEM. + VOWEL	son	ses
	FEM.	sa	
POSSESSOR PLURAL		NOUN POSSESSED	
		SINGULAR	PLURAL
our		notre	nos
your		votre	vos
their		leur	leurs

130

140

In English and in French possession can also be indicated with the possessive form: *Mary's dress, the teacher's book* → la robe **de** Marie, le livre **du** professeur (see *What is the Possessive?*, p. 22).

STUDY TIPS — POSSESSIVE ADJECTIVES

Pattern (see Tips *For Learning Word Forms*, p. 4)
It will be easy for you to establish a pattern if you follow our instructions under "Singular Possessor" and "Plural Possessor" (pp. 95-6).

Practice
1. Sort out your noun flashcards and select a few of the following:
   - all masculine nouns
   - feminine nouns beginning with a consonant
   - feminine nouns beginning with a vowel
2. Look at the French side and go through the cards saying the noun preceded by the correct forms of the possessive adjective. Concentrate on the singular forms **mon, ton, son** since they are the forms that change.

le jardin	*garden*
mon jardin, ton jardin, etc.	
la maison	*house*
ma maison, ta maison, etc.	
l'adresse (fem.)	*address*
mon adresse, ton adresse, etc.	

3. Look at the English side and go through the cards saying the French equivalent of the noun preceded by the correct form of the possessive adjective, again concentrating on the singular forms.

Flashcards

1. For review, create one card for each of the persons (1st, 2nd, and 3rd singular and plural) with an example of the different forms, including an example of a feminine singular noun beginning with a vowel.

1. mon livre, ma chaise, mes devoirs	*my (book, chair, homework)*
mon **idée** (fem.)	*my (idea)*
2. ton livre, ta chaise, tes devoirs,	*your*
3. votre (livre, chaise), vos (livres, chaises)	*your*

2. On the card for the 3rd person singular, to reinforce the fact that *his, her* and *its* can be either **son** or **sa**, write French sentences with 3rd pers. sing. possessive adjectives modifying masculine and feminine singular nouns.

Il prend son livre.	*He takes his (her) book.*
Elle prend son livre.	*She takes his (her) book.*
Il prend sa chaise.	*He takes his (her) chair.*
Elle prend sa chaise.	*She takes his (her) chair.*

WHAT IS AN INTERROGATIVE ADJECTIVE?

An **INTERROGATIVE ADJECTIVE** is a word that asks for information   1
about a noun.

> *Which* book do you want?
> asks information about the noun *book*

IN ENGLISH
The words *which* and *what* are interrogative adjectives when
they modify a noun and are used to ask for more information about that noun.

> *Which* teacher is teaching the course?
> *What* courses are you taking?   10

IN FRENCH
There is only one interrogative adjective, **quel.** As all French
adjectives it changes to agree in gender and number with the
noun it modifies. Therefore, start by analyzing the noun in
order to choose the appropriate form.

- noun modified is masculine singular → **quel**
   > *What book is on the table?*
   > **Livre** *(book)* → masculine singular
   > *what* → masculine singular → **quel**   20
   > **Quel** livre est sur la table?

- noun modified is masculine plural → **quels**
   > *What books are on the table?*
   > **Livres** *(books)* → masculine plural
   > *what* → masculine plural → **quels**
   > **Quels** livres sont sur la table?

- noun modified is feminine singular → **quelle**
   > *Which dress do you want?*
   > **Robe** *(dress)* → feminine singular
   > *which* → feminine singular → **quelle**   30
   > **Quelle** robe voulez-vous?

- noun modified is feminine plural → **quelles**
   > *Which dresses do you want?*
   > **Robes** *(dresses)* → feminine plural
   > *which* → feminine plural → **quelles**
   > **Quelles** robes voulez-vous?

In the sentences above, the noun that the interrogative adjective modifies is easy to identify because the noun and the adjective are next to one another. However, the noun modified is harder to identify when it is separated from the interrogative adjective. As you can see in the examples below, restructuring the sentences will help you identify the noun with which the interrogative adjective must agree.

> **What** *is your address?*
> Restructure: "*What address* is yours?"
> **Quelle** est votre adresse?
>   └──────────────┘
>   fem. sing.

> **Which** *are his favorite books?*
> Restructure: "*Which books* are his favorites?"
> **Quels** sont ses livres préférés?
>   └──────────────┘
>   masc. pl.

CAREFUL — The word *what* is not always an interrogative adjective. In the sentence *"What* is on the table?" it is an interrogative pronoun (see *What is an Interrogative Pronoun?*, p. 140). It is important that you distinguish one from the other because, in French, different words are used and they follow different rules.

WHAT IS A DEMONSTRATIVE ADJECTIVE?

A **DEMONSTRATIVE ADJECTIVE** is a word used to point out a noun or   1
to point to a noun.

> *This* book is interesting.
> |
> points out the noun *book*

IN ENGLISH

The demonstrative adjectives are ***this*** and ***that*** in the singular and ***these*** and ***those*** in the plural. They are rare examples of English adjectives agreeing in number with the noun
they modify: *this* changes to *these* and *that* changes to *those*
when they modify a plural noun.   10

SINGULAR	PLURAL
this cat	*these* cats
that man	*those* men

This and *these* refer to persons or objects near the speaker and
that and *those* refer to persons or objects away from the
speaker.

IN FRENCH

There is only one demonstrative adjective, **ce**. As all French
adjectives, it changes to agree in gender and number with   20
the noun it modifies. Therefore, start by analyzing the noun
in order to choose the appropriate form.

- noun modified is masculine singular and starts with a consonant → **ce**

    Ce livre est sur la table.
    > **Livre** *(book)* → masculine singular
    > *this* → masculine singular → **ce**

    ***This** (or **that**) book is on the table.*

- noun modified is masculine singular and starts with a   30
  vowel → **cet**

    Cet appartement est grand.
    > **Appartement** *(apartment)* → masculine singular, starts with a vowel
    > *this* → masculine singular before a vowel → **cet**

    ***This** (or **that**) apartment is large.*

- noun modified is feminine singular → **cette**

  Cette robe est jolie.

  > **Robe** *(dress)* → feminine singular
  > *this* → feminine singular → **cette**

  *This (or **that**) dress is pretty.*

- noun modified is plural → **ces**

  Ces livres sont sur la table.

  > **Livres** *(books)* → plural
  > *these* → plural → **ces**

  *These (or **those**) books are on the table.*

To distinguish between what is close to the speaker from what is far from the speaker, **-ci** *(here)* or **-là** *(there)* can be added after the noun.

> **Ces** livres-**ci** sont chers; **ces** livres-**là** ne sont pas chers.
> *These books (**here**) are expensive; **those** books (**there**) are not expensive.*

Notice the accent on **là** to distinguish it from the definite article **la** *(the)* without an accent (see p. 17).

WHAT IS AN ADVERB?

An **ADVERB** is a word that describes a verb, an adjective, or [1]
another adverb. It indicates manner, degree, time, place.[1]

> Jade drives *well.*
>   verb   adverb
>
> The house is *very* big.
>   adverb adjective
>
> The girl ran *too quickly.*
>   adverb   adverb

IN ENGLISH
[10]

There are different types of adverbs:

- an **ADVERB OF MANNER** answers the question *how?* Adverbs of manner are the most common and they are easy to recognize because they end with *-ly.*

  > Julia sings *beautifully.*
  > *Beautifully* describes the verb *sings*; it tells you how Julia sings.

- an **ADVERB OF DEGREE** answers the question *how much?*

  > Roger does *well* in class.

- an **ADVERB OF TIME** answers the question *when?*
[20]

  > He will arrive *soon.*

- an **ADVERB OF PLACE** answers the question *where?*

  > The children were left *behind.*

IN FRENCH

Most adverbs of manner can be recognized by the ending **-ment** that corresponds to the English ending *-ly.*

joli**ment**	*beautifully*
générale**ment**	*generally* [30]
heureuse**ment**	*happily*

Adverbs must be memorized as vocabulary items. Just like prepositions and conjunctions, adverbs are invariable; i.e., they never change form.

---

[1]In English and in French the structure for comparing adverbs is the same as the structure for comparing adjectives (see *What is Meant by Comparison of Adjectives?*, p. 91).

CAREFUL — While adverbs in English are usually placed after the subject of the sentence, in French they are usually placed after the verb.

> *I **always** study at home.*
> |
> subject

> J'étudie **toujours** à la maison.
> |
> verb

Consult your textbook for the placement of adverbs.

ADVERB OR ADJECTIVE? (see *What is an Adjective?*, p. 87)
Since adverbs are invariable and French adjectives must agree with the noun they modify, it is important that you distinguish one from the other. If the word in question modifies a noun it is an adjective; if it modifies a verb, an adjective, or another adverb it is an adverb.

> The student writes *good* English.
>> *Good* modifies the noun *English;* it is an adjective.
> The student writes *well.*
>> *Well* modifies the verb *writes;* it is an adverb.

When you write a sentence in French, always make sure that adjectives agree with the noun or pronoun they modify and that adverbs remain unchanged.

> *The **tall** girl walked **slowly**.*
>> *Tall* modifies the noun *girl;* it is an adjective. *Slowly* modifies the verb *walked* (it describes how the girl walked); it is an adverb.

> La **grande** fille marchait **lentement**.
>   fem. sing.   adverb

> *The **tall** boy walked **slowly**.*
>> *Tall* modifies the noun *boy;* it is an adjective. *Slowly* modifies the verb *walked* (it describes how the boy walked); it is an adverb.

> Le **grand** garçon marchait **lentement**.
>   masc. sing.   adverb

> *The **good** students speak French **well**.*
>> adjective   adverb
>> modifies   modifies
>> noun *student*   verb *speak*

> Les **bons** étudiants parlent **bien** le français.
>   adjective (masc. pl.)   adverb

For the comparative forms of *good* and *well* (**meilleur** and **mieux**), see p. 93.

CAREFUL — In spoken English adjectives are often used instead of adverbs. In French, however, the usage of an adjective for an adverb is incorrect; you must use an adverb.

*He speaks **real slow**.* → *He speaks **really slowly**.*

adj.	adj.		adverb	adverb	80
vrai	**lent**		modifies	modifies	
			verb	adverb	
			speaks	*really*	

Il parle **vraiment lentement**.

adverb   adverb

STUDY TIPS — ADVERBS

Flashcards (see *Tips for Learning Vocabulary*, p. 2)
1. Create flashcards for each French adverb you learn and its English equivalent.

souvent   *often*

2. When you learn the placement of adverbs in a sentence, add sample sentences illustrating their placement. (Refer to your textbook for the placement of adverbs.)

Elle parle souvent de son frère.   *She often speaks of her brother.*
Elle a souvent parlé de son frère.   *She often spoke of her brother.*

WHAT IS A CONJUNCTION?

1   A **CONJUNCTION** is a word that links two or more words or groups of words.

> He had to choose between good *and* evil.
> |
>   conjunction

> They left *because* they were bored.
> |
>   conjunction

IN ENGLISH

There are two kinds of conjunctions: coordinating and subordinating.

10   ■ a **COORDINATING CONJUNCTION** joins **WORDS**, **PHRASES**, i.e., a group of words without a verb, or **CLAUSES**, i.e., a group of words with a verb, to one another. The major coordinating conjunctions are *and, but, or, nor, for,* and *yet.*

> good *or* evil
> | |
> word   word

> over the river *and* through the woods
> ⌞   ⌟   ⌞   ⌟
>   phrase   phrase

> They invited us, *but* we couldn't go.
> ⌞   ⌟   ⌞   ⌟
20   clause   clause

In the last example, each of the two clauses, "they invited us" and "we couldn't go," expresses a complete thought; each clause is, therefore, a complete sentence that could stand alone. When a clause expresses a complete thought it is called a **MAIN CLAUSE**. Above, the coordinating conjunction *but* links two main clauses.

  ■ a **SUBORDINATING CONJUNCTION** joins a main clause to a dependent clause; it *subordinates* one clause to another. A **DEPENDENT CLAUSE** does not express a complete thought; it
30 is, therefore, not a complete sentence and cannot stand alone. There are various types of dependent clauses. A clause introduced by a subordinating conjunction is called a **SUBORDINATE CLAUSE**. Typical subordinating conjunctions are *before, after, since, although, because, if, unless, so that, while, that,* and *when.*

The subordinate clauses in the sentences below are underlined. As you can see, they are not complete sentences and each is introduced by a subordinating conjunction.

Although we were invited, we didn't go.

subordinating
conjunction

They left *because* they were bored.

subordinating
conjunction

He won't graduate, unless he starts studying.

subordinating
conjunction

IN FRENCH

Conjunctions must be memorized as vocabulary items. Just like adverbs and prepositions, conjunctions are invariable, i.e., they never change form. Be sure to memorize the conjunctions that are followed by the subjunctive mood instead of the indicative (see *What is the Subjunctive?*, p. 85).

STUDY TIPS — CONJUNCTIONS AND THE SUBJUNCTIVE

Flashcards (see *Tips for Learning Vocabulary*, p. 2)
1. Create flashcards indicating French conjunctions and their English equivalent.

    but   *mais*

2. When you learn the subjunctive, indicate whether the French conjunction is followed by a verb in the indicative or the subjunctive mood. Add an example as reinforcement.

    parce que (+ ind.)   *because*
    Il n'est pas sorti   *He didn't go out*
    parce qu'il est malade.   *because he is sick.*

    bien que (+ subj.)   *although*
    Il est sorti   *He went out*
    bien qu'il soit malade.   *although he is sick.*

Practice

Write a series of sentences using the various conjunctions. Make sure to put the following verb in the subjunctive, if the conjunction requires it.

CHAPTER

35

WHAT IS A PREPOSITION?

A **PREPOSITION** is a word with a meaning often related to time or space that links nouns to nouns, nouns to verbs, and different parts of a sentence to one another.

prepositional phrase
Roger has an appointment <i>after</i> school.
preposition   object of preposition

The noun or pronoun following the preposition is called the **OBJECT OF THE PREPOSITION**. The preposition plus its object is called a **PREPOSITIONAL PHRASE**.

IN ENGLISH

Prepositions normally indicate location, direction, or time.

- prepositions showing location or direction

    Roger was *in* the car.
    Jade put the books *on* the table.
    The students came directly *from* class.
    Julia went *to* school.

- prepositions showing time and date

    French people go on vacation *in* August.
    On Mondays, they go to the university.
    I'm meeting him *at* 4:30 today.
    We're studying *before* taking the exam.
    Most people work *from* nine to five.

Other frequently used prepositions are: *during, since, with, between, of, about.*

IN FRENCH

You will have to memorize prepositions as vocabulary, paying special attention to their meaning and use in French. Just like adverbs and conjunctions, prepositions are invariable; that is, they never change form.

CAREFUL — Prepositions can be tricky. Every language uses prepositions differently. Do not assume that the same preposition is used in French and in English, or even that a preposition will be needed in French when one is needed in English and vice versa.

ENGLISH	FRENCH
	CHANGE OF PREPOSITION
to be angry *with*	être fâché **contre** *(against)*
to be *on* the plane	être **dans** *(in)* l'avion

PREPOSITION	NO PREPOSITION
to wait *for*	attendre
to look *at*	regarder

NO PREPOSITION	PREPOSITION
to telephone	téléphoner à
to answer	répondre à

A dictionary will usually give you the verb and the preposition that follows it, when one is required. Do not translate an English verb + preposition with a word-for-word French equivalent (see *Consulting the dictionary*, p. 27).

STUDY TIPS — PREPOSITIONS

Flashcards (see *Tips for Learning Vocabulary*, p. 2)
Be careful when creating flashcards for prepositions: one English preposition can have several French equivalents and vice versa. Always learn a preposition in a short sentence illustrating its usage.

1. Prepositions indicating the position of one object or person in relation to another are the easiest to learn because the English preposition usually has only one French equivalent .

sur	*on top of*
Le livre est sur la table.	*The book is on the table.*
derrière	*behind, in back of*
Jean est derrière Marie.	*John is behind Mary.*

2. Prepositions such as *to, at, in* + place and *by, on, in* + a means of transportation have many French equivalents because they vary according to the noun that follows. Rather than creating separate cards for these prepositions, indicate them on the appropriate noun cards.

la ville	*town*
Je vais en ville.	*I'm going to town.*
la bibliothèque	*library*
Je vais à la bibliothèque.	*I'm going to the library.*
l'avion (masc.)	*plane*
Je vais en avion.	*I'm going by plane.*
la bicyclette	*bike*
Je vais à bicyclette.	*I'm going by bike.*

3. When you learn a verb that is usually followed by a preposition + noun, indicate the preposition on the verb card and write a short sentence to illustrate its use.

répondre (à)	*to answer*
Je réponds à sa lettre.	*I'm answering his letter.*

4. When you learn a verb that requires a preposition when it is followed by an infinitive, indicate the preposition on the verb card and write a short sentence to illustrate its use.

> décider de + infinitive   *to decide*
> J'ai décidé de partir.   *I decided to leave.*

Practice

1. Following the examples under 1 above, think of two objects (or persons) and write French sentences using prepositions placing the objects (or persons) in various positions in relation to one another.
2. Following the examples under 2 above, sort out the noun cards indicating a place or a means of transportation and create short sentences using them with the appropriate preposition.

WHAT IS AN OBJECT?

An **OBJECT** is a noun or pronoun indicating towards what or whom
the action of the verb is directed.

> Daniel writes a *letter*.
>   verb   object

> He speaks to *Julia*.
>   verb   object

> The boy left with *his father*.
>   verb   object

Verbs can be classified as to whether or not they require a direct
object (see below) to complete its meaning .

- a **TRANSITIVE VERB** (*v.t.* in the dictionary) is a verb that requires
a direct object to complete its meaning *(to give, to say)*.

  > The boy *threw* the ball.
  >   transitive

- an **INTRANSITIVE VERB** (*v.i.* in the dictionary) is a verb that
doesn't require a direct object to complete its meaning *(to
rain, to fall)*.

  > Daniel *slept*.
  >   intransitive

We will study the three types of objects separately: direct objects,
indirect objects, and objects of a preposition. Since noun and pronoun objects are identified the same way, we have limited the
examples in this section to noun objects (see *What is a Noun?*, p. 9).
For examples with pronoun objects see *What is a Direct Object Pronoun?*, p. 116, *What is an Indirect Object Pronoun?*, p. 119, and *What is
a Disjunctive Pronoun?*, p. 125. See also *What is a Preposition?*, p. 108.

DIRECT OBJECT
IN ENGLISH

A direct object is a noun or pronoun that receives the action
of the verb directly, without a preposition between the verb
and the noun or pronoun object. It answers the question
whom? or *what?* asked after the verb.[1]

---

[1]In this section, we will consider active sentences only (see *What is Meant by Active and Passive Voice?*, p. 165).

Alex writes *a letter*.
> Alex writes what? A letter.
> *A letter* is the direct object.

IN FRENCH

As in English, a direct object is a noun or pronoun that
receives the action of the verb directly, without a preposition.

> *Alex sees **Julia**.*
> Alex voit **Julia**.
>> No preposition separates **Julia** from the verb **voit** *(sees)*.
>> Therefore, **Julia** is a direct object.

> *Alex read **the book**.*
> Alex lit **le livre**.
>> No preposition separates **le livre** *(the book)* from the verb **lit** *(reads)*.
>> Therefore, **le livre** is a direct object.

As with English verbs, French verbs can be transitive or
intransitive depending on whether or not they are followed
by an object.

INDIRECT OBJECT
IN ENGLISH

An indirect object is a noun or pronoun that receives the
action of the verb indirectly, with the preposition *to* relating
it to the verb. It answers the question *to whom?* or *to what?*
asked after the verb.

> She spoke *to her friends*.
>> She spoke to whom? Her friends.
>> *Her friends* is the indirect object.

> He gave the painting *to the museum*.
>> He gave a painting to what? The museum.
>> *The museum* is the indirect object.

IN FRENCH

As in English, an indirect object is a noun or pronoun that
receives the action of the verb indirectly, with the preposition **à** *(to)* relating it to the verb.

> Elle a parlé **à ses amis**.
> *She spoke **to her friends**.*

> Il a donné le tableau **au musée**.
>> à + le → au
> *He gave the painting **to the museum**.*

Nouns that are indirect objects are easy to identify in French
because they are always preceded by the preposition **à**. Notice
the accent to distinguish it from *"a"* without an accent, *(has)*
the 3rd person singular present of the verb **avoir**.

SENTENCES WITH A DIRECT AND AN INDIRECT OBJECT

A sentence may contain both a direct object and an indirect object that can be either nouns or pronouns. In this section we shall only speak of sentences with nouns as direct and indirect objects. Consult your textbook for the word order of pronoun objects.

IN ENGLISH

When a sentence has both a direct and an indirect object, the following two word orders are possible:

1. subject (S) + verb (V) + indirect object (IO) + direct object (DO)

> Paul gave his sister a gift.
> S   V   IO   DO
>
> *Who* gave a gift? Paul.
> *Paul* is the subject.
>
> Paul gave *what?* A gift.
> *A gift* is the direct object.
>
> Paul gave a gift *to whom?* His sister.
> *His sister* is the indirect object.

2. subject + verb + direct object + *to* + indirect object

> Paul gave a gift *to* his sister.
> S   V   DO *to*   IO

The first structure, under 1, is the most common. However, because there is no *"to"* preceding the indirect object, it is more difficult to identify its function than in the second structure.

Regardless of the word order, the function of the words in the two sentences above is the same because they answer the same question: *to what?* and *to whom?* Be sure to ask questions to establish the function of words in a sentence.

IN FRENCH

Unlike in English, when a sentence has both a direct and an indirect object there is only one word order possible (structure 2): subject + verb + direct object + à *(to)* + indirect object.

> Paul a donné **un cadeau à sa soeur**.
> S   V   DO **à** IO
> *Paul gave **a gift to his sister.***
> *Paul gave **his sister a gift.***

OBJECT OF A PREPOSITION

IN ENGLISH

120   An object of a preposition is a noun or pronoun that receives the action of the verb through a preposition other than *to*. (Objects of the preposition *to* are considered indirect objects and are discussed above.) It answers the question *whom?* or *what?* asked after the preposition.

> Paul works *for Mary*.
>> Paul works *for whom?* Mary.
>> *Mary* is the object of the preposition *for*.

> The baby eats *with a spoon*.
>> The baby eats *with what?* A spoon.
>> *A spoon* is the object of the preposition *with*.

130

IN FRENCH

As in English, an object of a preposition is a noun or pronoun that receives the action of the verb through a preposition other than **à** *(to)*.

> Paul travaille **pour Marie**.
> *Paul works **for Mary**.*

> Le bébé mange **avec une cuillère**.
> *The baby eats **with a spoon**.*

140

RELATIONSHIP OF A VERB TO ITS OBJECT

The relationship between a verb and its object is often different in English and in French. For example, a verb may take a direct object in English and an indirect object in French, or an object of a preposition in English and a direct object in French. Therefore, when you learn a French verb it is important to find out if it is followed by a preposition and, if so, which one. Your textbook, as well as dictionaries, will indicate when a French verb needs a preposition before an object (see pp. 108-9).

150   Here are differences you are likely to encounter.

1. ENGLISH: object of a preposition → FRENCH: direct object

> *I am looking **for the book**.*
>> I am looking *for what?* The book.
>> *The book* is the object of the preposition *for*.
> Je cherche **le livre**.
>> *to look for* → **chercher**
>> Function in French: direct object

Many common verbs require an indirect object or an object 160
of a preposition in English, but a direct object in French.

*to listen **to***	écouter
*to look **at***	regarder
*to wait **for***	attendre

2. ENGLISH: direct object → FRENCH: indirect object

> *She phones **her friends** every day.*
>> She phones *whom*? Her friends.
>> *Her friends* is the direct object.
>
> Elle téléphone **à ses amis** tous les jours.
>> *to telephone* → **téléphoner à** 170
>> Function in French: indirect object

A few common verbs require a direct object in English and
an indirect object in French.

to obey	obéir **à**
to resemble	ressembler **à**
to ask (a person)	demander **à** (une personne)

3. ENGLISH: direct object → FRENCH: object of a preposition

> *The student enters **the classroom**.*
>> The student enters *what*? The classroom.
>> *The classroom* is the direct object. 180
>
> L'étudiant entre **dans la salle de classe**.
>> *to enter* → **entrer dans**
>> Function in French: object of the preposition **dans**

Your ability to recognize the three types of objects is essential.
With pronouns, for instance, a different French pronoun is
used for the English pronoun *him* depending on whether *him* is
a direct object (**le**) or an indirect object (**lui**).

SUMMARY

The different types of objects in a sentence can be identified by 190
establishing whether they answer a question that requires a
preposition or not and, if so, which one.

DIRECT OBJECT — An object that receives the action of the verb
directly, without a preposition.

INDIRECT OBJECT — An object that receives the action of the
verb indirectly, through the preposition *to*.

OBJECT OF A PREPOSITION — An object that receives the action
of the verb through a preposition other than *to*.

CAREFUL — Always identify the function of a word within the 200
language in which you are working; do not use English patterns
in French.

WHAT IS A DIRECT OBJECT PRONOUN?

1   A DIRECT OBJECT PRONOUN is a word that replaces a noun and
functions as a direct object of a verb (see *What is a Pronoun?*,
p. 31, and p. 111 in *What is an Object?*).

> Max saw *her*.
>> Max saw whom? Answer: Her.
>> *Her* is the direct object of the verb *saw*.

In this chapter we shall look at direct object pronouns. Other
object pronouns are studied in *What is an Indirect Object Pronoun?*, p. 119, and *What is a Disjunctive Pronoun?*, p. 125.

10   **IN ENGLISH**

Most object pronouns are different from subject pronouns.
The same form is used for direct object, indirect object, and
disjunctive pronouns.

	SUBJECT PRONOUN	OBJECT PRONOUN
SINGULAR		
1ST PERSON	I	me
2ND PERSON	you	you
3RD PERSON	he	him
	she	her
	it	it
PLURAL		
1ST PERSON	we	us
2ND PERSON	you	you
3RD PERSON	they	them

Let us look at two examples of direct object pronouns.

> He saw *him*.
> subject   direct object
> pronoun pronoun

> We met *them* at home.
30   subject   direct object
> pronoun pronoun

IN FRENCH

As in English, pronouns used as direct objects are different
from pronouns used as subjects. Unlike English, different
forms are used for direct and indirect object pronouns.

Let us look at French direct object pronouns to see how they are formed. We have divided them into two groups.

1ˢᵗ and 2ⁿᵈ person sing. and pl. (me, you, us)

The direct object pronouns of the 1ˢᵗ and 2ⁿᵈ persons have only one form per person. Just select the form you need from the chart below.

	SUBJECT	DIRECT OBJECT	SUBJECT	DIRECT OBJECT
SINGULAR 1ˢᵗ PERSON 2ⁿᵈ PERSON	je tu	me te	*I* *you*	*me* *you*
PLURAL 1ˢᵗ PERSON 2ⁿᵈ PERSON	nous vous	nous vous	*we* *you*	*us* *you*

To simplify our examples, we have used the verb **to see** *(voir)* because both the English and the French verbs take a direct object.

*Max sees **me**.*
1. Identify the verb: to see
2. What is the French equivalent: **voir**
3. Does the French verb need a preposition before an object: No
4. Function of pronoun in French: direct object
5. Selection: **me**

Max **me** voit.

*Max sees **you**.*
Max **te** voit.
Max **vous** voit.

*Max sees **us**.*
Max **nous** voit.

Establishing the function of **nous** and **vous** can be confusing. Not only are the same forms used as subject and object, but both subject and object pronouns are placed before the verb. In case of doubt, look at the verb. Remember that verbs agree with their subject. If **nous** is the subject, the verb will end in **-ons**; if it doesn't, **nous** is an object of some kind. The same is true with **vous**. If it is the subject of the verb, the ending of regular verbs will be **-ez**.

Nous vous voy**ons** tous les jours.
We see you everyday.

Vous nous voy**ez** tous les jours.
You see us everyday.

3ʳᵈ person sing. and pl. (him, her, it, them)

The direct object pronouns of the 3ʳᵈ person singular have a masculine and feminine form. The gender of *it* depends on the gender of its antecedent; that is, the noun that it is replacing. There is only one form for *them*.

	SUBJECT	DIRECT OBJECT	SUBJECT	DIRECT OBJECT
SINGULAR				
MASCULINE	il	**le**	*he, it*	**him, it**
FEMININE	elle	**la**	*she, it*	**her, it**
PLURAL				
MASCULINE	ils	**les**	*they*	**them**
FEMININE	elles			

For our examples we have again used the verb **to see** *(voir)* because both the English and French verbs take a direct object.

*Do you see Max? Yes, I see **him**.*
Voyez-vous Max? Oui, je **le** vois.

*Do you see Julia? Yes, I see **her**.*
Voyez-vous Julia? Oui, je **la** vois.

*Do you see the girls? Yes, I see **them**.*
Voyez-vous les jeunes filles? Oui, je **les** vois.

It as a direct object requires that you establish the gender of the noun *it* replaces (i.e., its antecedent).

*Do you see the book? Yes, I see **it**.*
　　1. Antecedent: *book* → **livre** → masculine
　　2. Gender of *it:* masculine → **le**
Voyez-vous le livre? Oui, je **le** vois.

*Do you see the table? Yes, I see **it**.*
　　1. Antecedent: *table* → **table** → feminine
　　2. Gender of *it:* feminine → **la**
Voyez-vous la table? Oui, je **la** vois.

Unlike English where direct object pronouns are placed after the verb, in French they are usually placed before the verb. Consult your textbook for the placement of pronouns.

CAREFUL — Make sure you establish the type of object appropriate for the French verb, not necessarily the same type as for the English verb (see *Relationship of a verb to its object*, p. 114-5). For object pronouns used with verbs in the affirmative imperative see p. 126 in *What is a Disjunctive Pronoun?*.

WHAT IS AN INDIRECT OBJECT PRONOUN?

An **INDIRECT OBJECT PRONOUN** is a word that replaces a noun and [1]
functions as an indirect object of a verb (see *What is a Pronoun?*,
p. 31, and p. 112 in *What is an Object?*).

> Roger spoke to *her*.
>> Roger spoke to whom? Answer: Her.
>> *Her* is the indirect object of the verb *spoke*.

In this chapter we shall look at indirect object pronouns. Other
object pronouns are studied in *What is a Direct Object Pronoun?*,
p. 116, and *What is a Disjunctive Pronoun?*, p. 125. [10]

IN ENGLISH

Most object pronouns are different from subject pronouns.
The same form is used for direct object, indirect object, and
disjunctive pronouns.

		SUBJECT PRONOUN	OBJECT PRONOUN
SINGULAR			
	1ST PERSON	I	me
	2ND PERSON	you	you
	3RD PERSON	he	him
		she	her
		it	it
PLURAL			
	1ST PERSON	we	us
	2ND PERSON	you	you
	3RD PERSON	they	them

[20]

Let us look at two examples of indirect object pronouns.

> He wrote a letter to *him*.
> subject — indirect object
> pronoun — pronoun

[30]

> They lent *them* a car.
> subject — indirect object
> pronoun — pronoun

IN FRENCH

As in English, pronouns used as indirect objects are different
from pronouns used as subjects. Unlike English, direct and
indirect object pronouns do not always have the same form.

Unlike nouns that are indirect objects, indirect objects pronouns are not preceded by the preposition **à** *(to)*. Let us look at French indirect object pronouns to see how they are formed. We have divided them into two groups.

1ˢᵗ and 2ⁿᵈ persons sing. and pl. (me, you, us)

The indirect object pronouns of the 1ˢᵗ and 2ⁿᵈ persons are the same as the direct object pronouns (see p. 117). Just select the form you need from the chart below.

	SUBJECT	**INDIRECT OBJECT**	**SUBJECT**	**INDIRECT OBJECT**
SINGULAR				
1ˢᵀ PERSON	je	**me**	*I*	*(to) me*
2ᴺᴰ PERSON	tu	**te**	*you*	*(to) you*
PLURAL				
1ˢᵀ PERSON	nous	**nous**	*we*	*(to) us*
2ᴺᴰ PERSON	vous	**vous**	*you*	*(to) you*

To simplify our examples, we have used the verb *to speak to* (**parler à**) because both the English and French verbs take an indirect object.

*Paul speaks **to me**.*
   1. Identify the verb: to speak
   2. What is the French equivalent: **parler**
   3. Is the French verb followed by **à**: Yes
   4. Function of the pronoun in French: indirect object
   5. Selection: **me**

Paul **me** parle.

*Paul speaks **to you**.*
Paul **te** parle.
Paul **vous** parle.

*Paul speaks **to us**.*
Paul **nous** parle.

Establishing the function of **nous** and **vous** can be confusing. Not only are the same forms used as subject and object, but both subject and object pronouns are placed before the verb. In case of doubt, look at the verb. Remember that verbs agree with their subject. If **nous** is the subject, the verb will end in **-ons**; if it doesn't, **nous** is an object of some kind. The same is true with **vous**. If it is the subject of the verb, the ending of regular verbs will be **-ez**.

Nous **vous** parlons.
*We are talking **to you**.*

Vous **nous** parlez.
*You are talking **to us**.*

3rd person sing. and pl. (him, her, it, them)

The indirect object pronouns of the 3rd persons have a different form depending on whether they refer a person or a thing or idea.

1. PERSON — a singular and a plural form

	SUBJECT	INDIRECT OBJECT	SUBJECT	INDIRECT OBJECT
SINGULAR MASCULINE FEMININE	il elle	lui	*him, it her, it*	*(to) him (to) her*
PLURAL MASCULINE FEMININE	ils elles	leur	*them*	*(to) them*

90

Are you speaking to Mary? Yes, I am speaking to her.
  1. Identify the verb: to speak
  2. What is the French equivalent: **parler**
  3. Is the French verb followed by à: Yes
  4. Function of the pronoun in French: indirect object
  5. Number of antecedent: singular *(Mary)*
  6. Selection: **lui**
Parlez-vous à Marie? Oui, je **lui** parle.

100

Are you speaking to Paul and Mary? Yes, I am speaking to them.
  1 - 4. See above.
  5. Number of antecedent: plural *(Paul and Mary)*
  6. Selection: **leur**
Parlez-vous à Paul et à Marie? Oui, je **leur** parle.

Since the 3rd person indirect object pronoun is the same for both genders, the only way you can tell if it refers to a male or female is from what has been said before.

110

2. THING AND IDEA — one form → y

Are you answering the letter? Yes, I am answering it.
  1. Identify the verb: to answer
  2. What is the French equivalent: **répondre**
  3. Is the French verb followed by à: Yes
  4. Function of the pronoun in French: indirect object
  5. Type of antecedent: thing *(the letter)*
  6. Selection: **y**
Répondez-vous à la lettre? Oui, j'**y** réponds.

120

Unlike English where indirect object pronouns are placed after the verb, in French they are usually placed before the verb. Consult your textbook for the placement of pronouns.

CAREFUL —Make sure you establish the type of object appropriate for the French verb, not necessarily the same type as for the English verb (see *Relationship of a verb to its object*, p. 114). For object pronouns used with verbs in the affirmative imperative see p. 126 in *What is a Disjunctive Pronoun?*

QUESTIONS TO ASK YOURSELF WHEN CHOOSING FRENCH DIRECT AND INDIRECT OBJECT PRONOUNS

130

DO → Direct object of the French verb
IO → Indirect object of the French verb

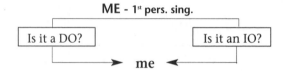

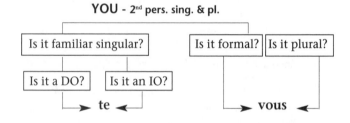

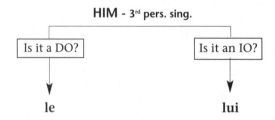

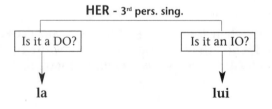

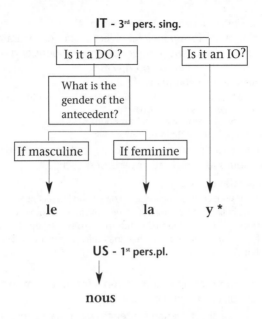

IT - 3ʳᵈ pers. sing.

Is it a DO ?   Is it an IO?

What is the gender of the antecedent?

If masculine   If feminine

le   **la**   **y** *

US - 1ˢᵗ pers.pl.

nous

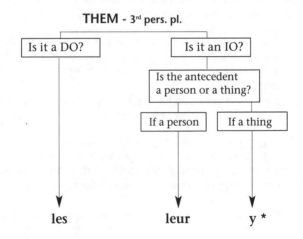

THEM - 3ʳᵈ pers. pl.

Is it a DO?   Is it an IO?

Is the antecedent a person or a thing?

If a person   If a thing

les   **leur**   **y** *

* Consult your textbook for other uses of "**y**".

Pattern (see *Tips For Learning Word Forms,* p. 4)
Learn the forms of direct and indirect object pronouns separately.
1. Look for similarities between direct object pronouns and other parts of speech. Refer to the charts on pp. 117-8.
   What similarities can you think of?
   - 1st & 2nd pers. sing.: initial **m-** and **t-** same as the initial letters of the possessive adjectives (**mon, ton**)
   - 1st & 2nd pers. pl.: same as subject pronouns
   - 3rd pers. sing. & pl.: same as definite articles
2. When you learn indirect object pronouns, look for similarities with direct object pronouns as well as other parts of speech.
   What similarities do you notice?
   - 1st, 2nd pers. sing. & pl.: same forms for direct and indirect object pronouns
   - 3rd pers. pl.: indirect object pronoun is the same as the singular form of the 3rd pers. pl. possessive adjective **leur**. (Careful: the possessive adjective has a singular and plural form (**leur, leurs**), while the indirect object pronoun has only one form, **leur**.)

Practice
1. Since function determines a pronoun's form, it is important to learn object pronouns in a sentence.
2. Write a series of short French sentences with masculine, feminine and plural direct and indirect objects. Rewrite the sentences replacing the object with the appropriate object pronoun.

Il donne le cadeau.	*He gives the gift.*
Il **le** donne.	*He gives **it**.*
Il parle à Marie.	*He speaks to Mary.*
*Il **lui** parle.*	*He speaks **to her**.*

Flashcards
1. On the subject pronoun flashcards, add sentences illustrating the pronoun's direct and indirect object forms.

il	*he, it*
Je **la (le)** vois.	*I see **her (him, it)**.*
Je **lui** donne un livre.	*I give **her (him)** a book.*

2. Review by going through the cards on the English side and creating French sentences illustrating the various forms.

WHAT IS A DISJUNCTIVE PRONOUN?

A **DISJUNCTIVE PRONOUN,** also known as **STRESSED** or **TONIC PRONOUN,**   1
functions primarily as a one-word answer to a question and as
an object of a preposition (see *What is a Pronoun?*, p. 31, and
p. 114 in *What is an Object?).*

> Who's doing the cooking? *Me.*
> Daniel arrived after *me.*

In this chapter we shall look at disjunctive pronouns. Other
types of pronouns are studied in *What is a Direct Object Pronoun?,*
p. 116, and *What is an Indirect Object Pronoun?*, p. 119.

IN ENGLISH   10

Most object pronouns are different from subject pronouns.
The same form is used for direct object, indirect object, and
disjunctive pronouns.

	SUBJECT PRONOUN	DISJUNCTIVE PRONOUN
SINGULAR		
1ST PERSON	I	me
2ND PERSON	you	you
3RD PERSON	he	him
	she	her
	it	it
PLURAL		
1ST PERSON	we	us
2ND PERSON	you	you
3RD PERSON	they	them

Disjunctive pronouns are used primarily in two instances:

1. in short answers when the identity of the person referred
   to is obvious from the context

> Who are you looking at? *Him.*
> Whom did he stay with? *Us.*   30

2. when the pronoun is an object of a preposition

> I'm staying *with **him**.*
> |
>   preposition
>
> He arrived *before **us**.*
> |
>   preposition

IN FRENCH

Most disjunctive pronouns, "LES PRONOMS PERSONNELS TONIQUES," have a different form than direct and indirect object pronouns.

		DISJUNCTIVE PRONOUNS	
SINGULAR			
1ST PERSON		moi	*me*
2ND PERSON		toi	*you*
3RD PERSON	{	lui	*him*
		elle	*her*
		—	*it*
PLURAL			
1ST PERSON		nous	*us*
2ND PERSON		vous	*you*
3RD PERSON	{	eux	*them* [men/men and women]
		elles	*them* [all women]

As in English, disjunctive pronouns are used in short answers when the identity of the person referred to is obvious from the context.

> *Who is there? **Me**.* [common in spoken English. Formal: "It is I."]
> Qui est là? **Moi**.

> *Whom do you want to see? **Him**.*
> Qui voulez-vous voir? **Lui**.
> ‎   masc. sing.

> *Whom do you want to see? **Her**.*
> Qui voulez-vous voir? **Elle**.
> ‎   fem. sing.

In French, disjunctive pronouns are also used:

- before a subject pronoun to replace the vocal emphasis used in English or to contrast one subject with another

> *What language do you speak? **I** speak French, **she** speaks English.*
> Quelle langue parlez-vous?
> **Moi, je** parle français, **elle, elle** parle anglais.
> ‎ disjunctive + subject   disjunctive + subject
> ‎ pronoun   pronoun   pronoun   pronoun

- as direct and indirect objects of the 1st and 2nd person singular of verbs in the affirmative imperative (see *What is the Imperative?*, p. 79)

> *Give **me** the book.*
> Donne-**moi** le livre.

> *Go to bed.*
> Couche-**toi**.

- as objects of a preposition (Remember, if the pronoun follows the preposition **à** it is an indirect object and takes an indirect object pronoun, not a disjunctive, see p. 112 in *What is an Object?*.)

> *Is the book for Alex?*   *No, it's **for me**.*
>   *No, it's **for you**.*
>   *No, it's **for us**.*
>> 1. Identify the verb: to be
>> 2. What is the French equivalent: **être**
>> 3. Is the French verb followed by a preposition? Yes.
>> 4. What preposition? **pour** *(for)*
>> 5. Function of pronoun in French: object of preposition
>> 6. Selection: **moi, toi (vous), nous**

> Est-ce que le livre est **pour** Alex? Non, il est **pour moi**.
>   Non, il est **pour toi (vous***)*.
>   Non, il est **pour nous**.

> *Is the book **behind** Alex ? Yes, it is **behind him**.*
>> 1. Identify the verb: to be
>> 2. What is the French equivalent: **être**
>> 3. Is the French verb followed by a preposition? Yes
>> 4. What preposition? **derrière** *(behind)*
>> 5. Function of pronoun in French: object of preposition
>> 6. Gender of antecedent: masculine *(Alex)*
>> 7. Selection: **lui**

> Est-ce que le livre est **derrière** Alex? Oui, il est **derrière lui**.

> *Is the book behind Julia? Yes, it is **behind her**.*
>> 1 - 5. See above.
>> 6. Gender of antecedent: feminine *(Julia)*
>> 7. Selection: **elle**

> Est-ce que le livre est **derrière** Julia? Oui, il est **derrière elle**.

> *Is Roger eating **with the boys**? Yes he is eating **with them**.*
>> 1. Identify the verb: to eat
>> 2. What is the French equivalent: **manger**
>> 3. Is the French verb followed by a preposition? Yes
>> 4. What preposition? **avec** *(with)*
>> 5. Function of pronoun in French: object of preposition
>> 6. Gender of antecedent: masculine *(boys)*
>> 7. Selection: **eux**

> Est-ce que Roger mange **avec** les garçons? Oui, il mange **avec eux**.

> *Is Roger eating **with the girls**? Yes he is eating **with them**.*
>> 1 - 5. See above.
>> 6. Gender of antecedent: feminine *(girls)*
>> 7. Selection: **elles**

> Est-ce que Roger mange **avec** les filles? Oui, il mange **avec elles**.

EXCEPTION: When *it* or *them* (referring to a thing or an idea) are objects of the preposition **de** *(of)*, the pronoun **en** is used.

*I liked the book so I am going to talk **about it**.*
1. Identify the verb: to talk
2. What is the French equivalent: **parler**
3. Is the French verb followed by **de**: Yes
4. Function of pronoun in French: object of preposition **de**
5. Type of antecedent: thing *(book)*
6. Selection: **en** (replaces **de** + pronoun)

J'ai aimé le livre alors je vais **en** parler.

130

*I liked these books so I am going to talk **about them**.*
1 - 6. See above.

J'ai aimé ces livres alors je vais **en** parler.

Consult your textbook for other uses of disjunctive pronouns and the pronoun **en**.

CAREFUL —Make sure you establish the type of object appropriate for the French verb, not necessarily the same type as for the English verb (see *Relationship of a verb to its object*, p. 114).

140 **SUMMARY OF FRENCH OBJECT PRONOUNS**
DO → Direct object of the French verb
IO → Indirect object of the French verb
OP → Object of a preposition of the French verb
DP → Disjunctive pronoun
Imp. → Affirmative imperative

ME — 1ˢᵗ pers. sing.
1. DO/IO .... **me**
   DO: *He sees **me**.* → Il **me** voit.
   IO: *He speaks to **me**.* → Il **me** parle.
2. OP/DP .... **moi**
   OP: *He speaks with **me**.* → Il parle avec **moi**.
   Imp. + DO → DP: *Catch **me**.* → Attrape-**moi**.
   Imp. + IO → DP: *Speak to **me**.* → Parle-**moi**.
   Imp. + OP/DP: *Speak with **me**.* → Parle avec **moi**.

YOU — 2ⁿᵈ pers. sing./pl.
1. familiar sing.
   ■ DO/IO .... **te**
      DO: *He sees **you**.* → Il **te** voit.
      IO: *He speaks to **you**.* → Il **te** parle.
   ■ OP/DP .... **toi**
      OP: *He speaks with **you**.* → Il parle avec **toi**.
      Imp. + DO → DP: *Get up.* → Lève-**toi**.

2. familiar pl. and formal sing. & pl. .... **vous**

 DO: *He sees you.* → Il **vous** voit.

 IO: *He speaks to you.* → Il **vous** parle.

 OP: *He speaks with you.* → Il parle avec **vous**.

 Imp. + DO → DP: *Get up.* → Levez-**vous**.

HIM — 3ᴿᴰ pers. sing.

1. DO .... **le**

 DO: *She sees him.* → Elle **le** voit.

 Imp. + DO: *Catch him.* Attrape-**le**.

2. IO/OP .... **lui**

 IO: *She speaks to him.* → Elle **lui** parle.

 OP: *She speaks with him.* → Elle parle avec **lui**.

 Imp. + IO: *Speak to him.* → Parle-**lui**.

HER — 3ᴿᴰ pers. sing.

1. DO .... **la**

 DO: *He sees her.* → Il **la** voit.

 Imp. + DO: *Catch her.* Attrape-**la**.

2. IO .... **lui**

 IO: *He speaks to her.* → Il **lui** parle.

 Imp. + IO: *Speak to her.* → Parle-**lui**.

3. OP .... **elle**

 OP: *He speaks with her.* → Il parle avec **elle**.

IT — 3ᴿᴰ pers. sing.

1. DO

 ■ masc. antecedent .... **le**

 DO: *He sees it.* → Il **le** voit. [le livre]

 Imp. + DO: *Catch it.* Attrape-**le**.

 ■ fem. antecedent .... **la**

 DO: *He sees it.* → Il **la** voit. [la balle]

 Imp. + DO: *Catch it.* Attrape-**la**.

2. IO .... **y**

 He answers it. → Il **y** répond. [répondre à]

3. OP **de** .... **en**

 He talks about it. → Il **en** parle.

US — 1ˢᵗ pers. pl. .... **nous**

 DO: *He sees us.* → Il **nous** voit.

 IO: *He speaks to us* → Il **nous** parle.

 OP: *He speaks with us.* → Il parle avec **nous**.

 Imp. + DO: *Let's [us] get up.* → Levons-**nous**.

THEM — 3RD pers. pl.

1. DO (antecedent a person/thing) .... **les**
   DO: *He sees **them** [his friends/keys].* → Il **les** voit.
   Imp. + DO: *Catch **them**.* → Attrape-**les**.

2. IO (antecedent a person) .... **leur**
   IO: *He answers **them**.* Il **leur** répond. [répondre à]
   Imp. + IO: *Speak **to them**.* Parle-**leur**.

3. IO (antecedent a thing) .... **y**
   *He answers **them** [the letters].* → Il **y** répond. [répondre à]

4. OP including **de** (antecedent a person)
   ■ masc. antecedent .... **eux**
   *He speaks with **them** [his brothers].* → Il parle avec **eux**.
   Imp. + OP: *Speak with **them**.* → Parle avec **eux**.
   *He speaks about **them*** → Il parle d'**eux**.

   ■ fem. antecedent .... **elles**
   *He speaks with **them** [his sisters].* → Il parle avec **elles**.
   Imp. + OP: *Speak with **them**.* → Parle avec **elles**.
   *He speaks about **them**.* → Il parle d'**elles**.

5. OP **de** (antecedent a thing) .... **en**
   *He speaks about **them** [his classes].* → Il **en** parle.

Consult your textbook for the placement of pronoun objects with affirmative and negated verbs.

WHAT ARE REFLEXIVE PRONOUNS AND VERBS?

A **REFLEXIVE VERB** is a verb that is accompanied by a pronoun,   1
called a **REFLEXIVE PRONOUN**, that serves *to reflect* the action of the
verb back to the subject.

> subject = reflexive pronoun → the same person
> She *cut herself* with the knife.
>   reflexive verb

IN ENGLISH

Many regular verbs can take on a reflexive meaning by
adding a reflexive pronoun.

> The child *dresses* the doll.   10
>   regular verb
>
> The child *dresses herself.*
>   verb + reflexive pronoun

Reflexive pronouns end with *-self* in the singular and
-selves in the plural.

		SUBJECT PRONOUN + VERB	+	REFLEXIVE PRONOUN
SINGULAR				
1ST PERSON		I	wash	myself
2ND PERSON		you	wash	yourself
		he	washes	himself
3RD PERSON	{	she	washes	herself
		it	washes	itself
PLURAL				
1ST PERSON		we	wash	ourselves
2ND PERSON		you	wash	yourselves
3RD PERSON		they	wash	themselves

20

As the subject changes so does the reflexive pronoun, because
they both refer to the same person or object.   30

> I cut *myself.*
> *Julia and Jade* blamed *themselves* for the accident.

Although the subject pronoun *you* is the same for the singular and plural, there is a difference in the reflexive pronouns: *yourself* is used when you are speaking to one person
(singular) and *yourselves* is used when you are speaking to
more than one (plural).

Max, did you make *yourself* a sandwich?
Children, make sure you wash *yourselves* properly.

Reflexive verbs can be in any tense: *I wash myself, I washed myself, I will wash myself,* etc.

IN FRENCH

As in English, reflexive verbs, "LES VERBES RÉFLÉCHIS" also known as "LES VERBES PRONOMINAUX," are formed with a verb and a reflexive pronoun.

Here are the French reflexive pronouns:

SINGULAR

1ST PERSON	me	*myself*
2ND PERSON	te	*yourself*
3RD PERSON	se	*himself, herself, itself, oneself*

PLURAL

1ST PERSON	nous	*ourselves*
2ND PERSON	vous	*yourself, yourselves*
3RD PERSON	se	*themselves*

In the dictionary, reflexive verbs are listed under the regular verb. For instance, under **laver** *(to wash)* you will also find **se laver** *(to wash oneself).*

Look at the conjugation of **se laver**. Notice two things: 1. as in English, the reflexive pronoun changes according to the person of the conjugation, and 2. unlike in English, the reflexive pronoun is placed before the verb.

	SUBJECT PRONOUN +	REFLEXIVE PRONOUN +	VERB
SINGULAR			
1ST PERSON	je	me	lave
2ND PERSON	tu	te	laves
3RD PERSON	il elle on	se	lave
PLURAL			
1ST PERSON	nous	nous	lavons
2ND PERSON	vous	vous	lavez
3RD PERSON	ils elles	se	lavent

Reflexive verbs can be conjugated in all tenses. The subject and reflexive pronouns remain the same, regardless of the tense of the verb: **je me** *laverai* (**futur**); **je me** *suis lavé* (**passé composé**). In compound tenses reflexive verbs are conjugated with the auxiliary **être**, but the rules of agreement of the past participle of reflexive verbs are different from the rules of agreement of the past participle of regular verbs (see pp. 64-5). Be sure to consult your French textbook for the rules of agreement of the past participle of reflexive verbs.

Regular verbs that use the auxiliary **être** *(to be)* in compound tenses cannot be made reflexive. However, regular verbs that use the auxiliary **avoir** *(to have)* in compound tenses are made reflexive with the use of the auxiliary **être.**

REGULAR VERB	REFLEXIVE VERB
Il **a coupé** le pain.	Il **s'est coupé** en se rasant.
*He **cut** the bread.*	*He **cut himself** shaving.*
Roger **a acheté** un livre.	Roger **s'est acheté** un livre.
*Roger **bought** a book.*	*Roger **bought himself** a book.*
Marie **a fait** le dîner.	Marie **s'est fait** une robe.
*Mary **made** dinner.*	*Mary **made herself** a dress.*

Reflexive verbs are common in French. There are many expressions that are not reflexive in English, but whose French equivalent is a reflexive verb. You will have to memorize these idiomatic expressions.

to get up	se lever *(to get oneself up)*
to go to bed	se coucher *(to put oneself to bed)*
to wake up	se réveiller *(to wake oneself up)*
to be bored	s'ennuyer *(to bore oneself)*
to have a good time	s'amuser *(to amuse oneself)*
to make a mistake	se tromper *(to mistake oneself)*
to stop	s'arrêter *(to stop oneself)*
to take a walk	se promener *(to walk oneself)*

In all the examples above, the French reflexive pronouns have a meaning equivalent to the English reflexive pronouns listed on p. 131 *(myself, yourself, himself,* etc.). That is not always the case. French reflexive pronouns can also indicate reciprocal action.

RECIPROCAL ACTION
IN ENGLISH

English uses a regular verb followed by the expression "each other" to express reciprocal action, that is, an action between two or more persons or things.

The dog and the cat looked at *each other.*

> The expression "each other" tells us that the action of *looking* was reciprocal, i.e., the dog looked at the cat and the cat looked at the dog.

Our children call *each other* every day.

> The expression "each other" tells us that the action of *calling* is reciprocal, i.e., the various children call one another every day.

Since reciprocal verbs require that more than one person or thing be involved, the verb is always plural.

IN FRENCH

French uses reflexive pronouns to express an action that is reciprocal.

> Le chien et le chat **se** regardaient.
> *The dog and the cat looked at **each other**.*

> Nos enfants **se** téléphonent tous les jours.
> *Our children call **each other** every day.*

The meaning of a French reflexive pronoun can be ambiguous.

> Les danseurs **se regardent**.
> *The dancers **look at themselves**.* → REFLEXIVE
> *The dancers **look at each other**.* → RECIPROCAL

One way to avoid ambiguity, and to indicate that the meaning is reciprocal rather than reflexive, is to add an expression equivalent to "each other," such as "**l'un l'autre**" (singular) or "**les uns les autres**" (plural).

> Le chien et le chat **se** regardent **l'un l'autre**.
> sing.　　　sing.　　　　　　sing.
> *The dog and the cat look at **each other**.*

> Les danseurs **se** regardent **les uns les autres**.
> plural　　　　　　　　　plural
> *The dancers look at **each other**.*

Consult your textbook for detailed explanations.

WHAT IS A POSSESSIVE PRONOUN?

A **POSSESSIVE PRONOUN** is a word that replaces a noun and indi- cates the possessor of that noun. The word *possessive* comes from *possess*, to own.

> Whose house is that? It's *mine*.
> > *Mine* replaces the noun *house*, the object possessed, and shows who possesses it, "me."

IN ENGLISH

Here is a list of the possessive pronouns:

SINGULAR POSSESSOR

1ST PERSON		mine
2ND PERSON		yours
3RD PERSON	MASCULINE	his
	FEMININE	hers

PLURAL POSSESSOR

1ST PERSON	ours
2ND PERSON	yours
3RD PERSON	theirs

Possessive pronouns only refer to the possessor, not to the object possessed.

> My car is red; what color is Paul's? *His* is blue.
> > 3rd pers. masc. sing.

> Paul's car is blue. What color is yours? *Mine* is white.
> > 1st pers. sing.

> > Although the object possessed is the same *(car)*, different pos- sessive pronouns *(his* and *mine)* are used because the possessors are different *(Paul* and *me)*.

> Is that Paul's house? Yes, it is *his*.
> Are those Paul's keys? Yes, they are *his*.
> > Although the objects possessed are different *(house* and *keys)*, the same possessive pronoun *(his)* is used because the possessor is the same *(Paul)*.

IN FRENCH

Like in English, a French possessive pronoun refers to the possessor. Unlike in English, it also agrees, like all French pro- nouns, in gender and number with its **ANTECEDENT**, that is with the person or thing possessed. In addition, the possessive pronoun is preceded by a definite article that also agrees in gender and number with the antecedent.

Let us look at French possessive pronouns to see how they are formed. We have divided the French possessive pronouns into two groups.

SINGULAR POSSESSOR (1ST, 2ND AND 3RD PERS. SING.)
mine, yours (tu-form), his/hers

Each of these possessive pronouns has four forms depending on the gender and number of the antecedent. To choose the proper form follow these steps.

1. Indicate the possessor. This will be shown by the first letter of the possessive pronoun. (They are the same initial letters as the possessive adjectives, see *What is a Possessive Adjective?*, p. 94.)

mine	**m-**
yours (tu-form)	**t-**
his }	**s-**
hers	

2. Establish the gender and number of the antecedent.
3. Choose the definite article and the ending that corresponds to the antecedent's gender and number.

- noun possessed is masculine singular → **le** + first letter of the possessor + **-ien**

A qui est ce **livre?**	C'est **le mien**.
masculine singular	C'est **le tien**.
	C'est **le sien**.
*Whose **book** is that?*	*It is **mine**.*
	*It is **yours**.*
	*It is **his (hers)**.*

- noun possessed is feminine singular → **la** + first letter of the possessor + **-ienne**

A qui est cette **lettre?**	C'est **la mienne**.
feminine singular	C'est **la tienne**.
	C'est **la sienne**.
*Whose **letter** is that?*	*It is **mine**.*
	*It is **yours**.*
	*It is **his (hers)**.*

- noun possessed is masculine plural → **les** + first letter of the possessor + **-iens**

A qui sont ces **livres?**	Ce sont **les miens**.
masculine plural	Ce sont **les tiens**.
	Ce sont **les siens**.

*Whose **books** are those?*   *They are **mine**.*
*They are **yours**.*
*They are **his (hers)**.*

- noun possessed is feminine plural → **les** + first letter of the possessor + **-iennes**

    A qui sont ces **lettres?**   Ce sont **les miennes**.
        |
    feminine plural   Ce sont **les tiennes**.
                              Ce sont **les siennes**.
    *Whose **letters** are those?*   *They are **mine**.*
                                   *They are **yours**.*
                                   *They are **his (hers)**.*   90

3. Select the proper form according to the two steps above.

Let us apply these steps to some examples.

    *Julia is looking at her photos. Daniel is looking at **yours**.*
       1. Possessor: *yours* [familiar] → 2nd pers. sing. → **t-**
       2. Antecedent: **photos** *(photos)* → feminine plural
       3. Add definite article & ending: **les** + **t-** + **-iennes**
    Julia regarde ses photos. Daniel regarde **les tiennes**.

    *Lend me your book. No, I'll lend you **hers**.*   100
       1. Possessor: *hers* → 3rd pers. sing. → **s-**
       2. Antecedent: **livre** *(book)* → masculine singular
       3. Add definite article & ending: **le** + **s-** + **-ien**
    Prêtez-moi votre livre. Non, je vous prêterai **le sien**.

PLURAL POSSESSOR (1ST, 2ND AND 3RD PERS. PL.)
ours, yours (vous-form), theirs

Each of these possessive pronouns has two forms, a singular and a plural, depending on the number of the antecedent. The definite article that precedes the pronoun agrees with the gender as well as with the number of the antecedent. To   110 choose the proper form, follow these steps:

1. Indicate the possessor.

    ours   **nôtre**
    yours   **vôtre**
    theirs   **leur**

2. Establish the gender and number of the antecedent.
3. Choose the definite article that corresponds to the antecedent's gender and number.
4. If the antecedent is plural, add an "**s**" to the possessive   120 pronoun.

Let us apply these steps to some examples.

*He read my letter. Did he read **yours?***
    1. Possessor: *yours* [formal]→ 2ⁿᵈ pers. pl. → **vôtre**
    2. Antecedent: **lettre** *(letter)* → feminine singular → **la**
    3. Selection: **la vôtre**
Il a lu ma lettre. A-t-il lu **la vôtre?**

*I do not have my books, but Alex and Jade have **theirs.***
    1. Possessor: *theirs* → 3ʳᵈ pers. pl. → **leur**
    2. Antecedent: **livres** *(books)* → plural → **les**
    3. Make possessive pronoun plural: **les + leur + s**
Je n'ai pas mes livres, mais Alex et Jade ont **les leurs.**

Although **vôtre** is classified as "second person plural," it can refer to just one person when used as a formal form of address (see p. 34).

SUMMARY

Here is a chart you can use as a reference.

POSSESSOR SINGULAR		NOUN POSSESSED	
		SINGULAR	PLURAL
mine	MASC.	le mien	les miens
	FEM.	la mienne	les miennes
yours (**tu**-form)	MASC.	le tien	les tiens
	FEM.	la tienne	les tiennes
his, hers	MASC.	le sien	les siens
	FEM.	la sienne	les siennes
POSSESSOR PLURAL		NOUN POSSESSED	
		SINGULAR	PLURAL
ours	MASC.	le nôtre	les nôtres
	FEM.	la nôtre	
yours (**vous**- form)	MASC.	le vôtre	les vôtres
	FEM.	la vôtre	
theirs	MASC.	le leur	les leurs
	FEM.	la leur	

STUDY TIPS — POSSESSIVE PRONOUNS

Pattern (see *Tips For Learning Word Forms*, p. 4)
1. It will be easy for you to establish a pattern if you follow our instructions above under "Singular Possessor" and "Plural Possessor" (pp. 136-8).
2. Note the circumflex over the "o" in **nôtre** and **vôtre** which, along with the definite article, distinguishes these plural possessive pronouns from the plural forms of the possessive adjective **notre** and **votre** (see p. 96).

Practice

1. You can use the same selection of noun flashcards you used to practice possessive adjectives (see p. 98).
2. Look at the French side and go through the cards replacing the nouns with the correct form of the possessive pronoun. Concentrate on the singular forms **le mien, le tien, le sien** since they are the forms that change.

un jardin	*garden*
le mien, le tien, etc.	*mine*
une maison	*house*
la mienne, la tienne, etc.	*mine*

3. Write short questions in French requiring an answer with a possessive pronoun.

Est-ce que c'est ton livre?	*Is that your book?*
Oui, c'est le mien.	*Yes, it is mine.*
Est-ce que ce sont tes clés?	*Are those your keys?*
Oui, ce sont les miennes.	*Yes, they are mine.*

4. Give negative answers to the questions you wrote under 3 above so that the answer will require a different possessive pronoun from the one given above.

Est-ce que c'est ton livre?	*Is that your book?*
Non, c'est le sien.	*No, it is hers (his).*
Est-ce que ce sont tes clés?	*Are those your keys?*
Non, ce sont les leurs.	*No, they are theirs.*

Flashcards

1. For review, create one card per person (1st, 2nd, and 3rd person singular and plural) with an example of the different forms.

   le mien, la mienne, les miens, les miennes   *mine*

2. On the cards for the 3rd person singular and plural, to reinforce the fact that *his* or *hers* can be either **le sien, la sienne, les siens, les siennes**, write French questions requiring answers equivalent to *his* and *hers*.

Est-ce que c'est le livre de Marie (Paul)?	*Is it Mary's (Paul's) book?*
Oui, c'est le sien.	*Yes, it's hers (his).*
Est-ce que ce sont les livres de Marie (Paul)?	*Are they Mary's (Paul's) books?*
Oui, ce sont les siens.	*Yes, they're hers (his).*
Est-ce que c'est la clé de Marie (Paul)?	*Is it Mary's (Paul's) key?*
Oui, c'est la sienne.	*Yes, it's hers (his).*

CHAPTER

42

WHAT IS AN INTERROGATIVE PRONOUN?

1   An **INTERROGATIVE PRONOUN** is a word that replaces a noun and introduces a question. The word *interrogative* comes from *interrogate,* to question.

> *Who* is coming for dinner?
> replaces a person

> *What* did you eat for dinner?
> replaces a thing

In English and in French a different interrogative pronoun is used depending on whether it refers to a person (human beings, animals) or a thing (objects, ideas). Also, the form of the interrogative pronoun often changes according to its function in the sentence: subject, direct object, indirect object, or object of a preposition. We shall look at each function separately.

SUBJECT (see *What is a Subject?*, p. 29)

IN ENGLISH

A different interrogative pronoun is used depending on whether it refers to a person or a thing.

PERSON → *who*

20
> *Who* speaks French?
> subject verb 3ʳᵈ pers. sing.

THING → *what*

> *What* is on the table?
> subject verb 3ʳᵈ pers. sing.

An interrogative pronoun used as subject is followed by the verb in the 3ʳᵈ person singular.

IN FRENCH

As in English, a different interrogative pronoun is used
30   depending on whether it refers to a person or a thing.

PERSON → **qui** + verb *or* **qui est-ce qui** + verb

> **Qui** parle français?
> **Qui est-ce qui** parle français?
> verb 3ʳᵈ pers. sing.
> ***Who* speaks French?**

THING — **Qu'est-ce qui** + verb

> **Qu'est-ce qui** est sur la table?
> verb 3ʳᵈ pers. sing.
> *What is on the table?* 40

As in English, an interrogative pronoun used as subject is followed by a verb in the 3ʳᵈ person singular.

DIRECT OBJECT (see p. 111 in *What is an Object?*)

IN ENGLISH

A different interrogative pronoun is used depending on whether it refers to a person or a thing.

PERSON → *whom*

> *Whom* do you know here? 50
> direct object subject

In spoken English, *whom* is often replaced by *who* (ex: "*Who* do you know here?"). It is only by analyzing the sentence that you will be able to establish the function of the interrogative pronoun.

THING → *what*

> *What* do you want?
> direct object subject

60

IN FRENCH

Regardless of the function of the French interrogative pronoun, the forms with **est-ce que** take the normal word order: noun or pronoun subject + verb, whereas the other forms take the inverted verb: verb + pronoun subject (rarely used with a noun subject).

As in English, a different interrogative pronoun is used depending on whether it refers to a person or a thing.

PERSON → **qui est-ce que** + subject + verb *or* **qui** + verb + subject pronoun 70

> **Qui est-ce que** vous connaissez?
> subject + verb
> **Qui** connaissez-vous?
> verb + subject pronoun
> *Who(m) do you know?*

THING → **qu'est-ce que** + subject + verb *or* **que** + verb + subject pronoun

80

> **Qu'est-ce que** vous voulez?
> subject + verb
>
> **Que** voulez-vous?
> verb + subject pronoun
>
> *What do you want?*

INDIRECT OBJECT AND OBJECT OF A PREPOSITION (see p. 112, and p. 114 in *What is an Object?*)

IN ENGLISH

The same form of the interrogative pronoun is used as an indirect object and as an object of a preposition. However, a different interrogative pronoun is used depending on whether it refers to a person or a thing.

90

PERSON → ***Whom, who*** (see **Restructuring sentences** below)

> *Who did you speak to?* →
> *To whom did you speak?*
> indirect object
>
> *Who did you get the book from?* →
> *From whom did you get the book?*
> object of preposition *from*

100

THING → ***what***

> *What did you pay with?* →
> *With what did you pay?*
> object of preposition *with*

Restructuring sentences with dangling prepositions (see p. 153-4)

It is difficult to identify an English interrogative pronoun functioning as an indirect object or as an object of a preposition for two reasons: 1. the interrogative pronoun is often separated from the preposition of which it is the object; in that case the preposition is called a **DANGLING PREPOSITION,** and 2. in spoken English the direct object *whom* is often replaced by *who.*

110

> *Who(m) did you speak to?*
> interr. pronoun   dangling preposition
>
> *Who(m) did you get the book from?*
> interr. pronoun   dangling preposition

To establish if an interrogative pronoun is an indirect object or an object of a preposition, you will have to change the structure of the sentence so that the preposition is placed before the interrogative pronoun. This restructuring will not only make it easier for you to identify the function of the pronoun, but it will also establish the word order for the French sentence.

The following sentences have been restructured to avoid a dangling preposition.

> *Who* are you giving the book *to?* →
> interr. pronoun   dangling preposition
> *To whom* are you giving the book?
> indirect object

> *What* are you contributing *to?* →
> interr. pronoun   dangling preposition
> *To what* are you contributing?
> indirect object

> *Who* are you going out *with?* →
> interr. pronoun   dangling preposition
> *With whom* are you going out?
> object of the preposition *with*

> *What* are you writing *with?* →
> interr. pronoun   dangling preposition
> *With what* are you writing?
> object of the preposition *with*

IN FRENCH

As in English, the same form of the interrogative pronoun is used as an indirect object (always preceded by the preposition **à**) and as an object of a preposition (always preceded by a preposition other than **à**). As in English, a different interrogative pronoun is used depending on whether it refers to a person or a thing.

PERSON → preposition + **qui est-ce que** + subject + verb *or* preposition + **qui** + verb + subject pronoun

> **A qui est-ce que** vous donnez le livre?
>   subject + verb
> **A qui** donnez-vous le livre?
>   verb + subject pronoun
> *To whom are you giving the book? [Who are you giving the book to?]*
> indirect object

Avec qui est-ce que vous sortez?

        subject + verb

160

Avec qui sortez-vous?

        verb + subject pronoun

With whom *are you going out?* [***Who*** *are you going out* ***with?***]

object of preposition *with*

THING → preposition + **quoi est-ce que** + subject + verb *or*
preposition + **quoi** + verb + subject pronoun

A quoi est-ce que vous contribuez?

        subject + verb

170

A quoi contribuez-vous?

        verb + subject pronoun

To what *are you contributing?* [***What*** *are you contributing* ***to?***]

indirect object

Avec quoi est-ce que vous écrivez?

        subject + verb

Avec quoi écrivez-vous?

        verb + subject pronoun

With what *are you writing?* [***What*** *are you writing* ***with?***]

object of the preposition *with*

180

CAREFUL — Remember: some French verbs take direct objects, while the equivalent English verbs take an indirect object and vice versa (see *Relationship of a verb to its object*, pp. 114-5). Determine the function of the pronoun in French.

SUMMARY

To choose the correct form of French interrogative pronouns, proceed with the following three steps:

1. Determine the function of the interrogative pronoun in the French sentence.

190

2. Establish whether the pronoun refers to a person or a thing.

3. Refer to the chart below.

	Subject	Direct object	Indirect object and object of a preposition
PERSON	*who* qui est-ce qui qui	*who(m)* qui est-ce que qui (+ inversion)	*preposition + who(m)* prép. + qui est-ce que prép. + qui (+ inversion)
THING	*what* qu'est-ce qui	*what* qu'est-ce que que (+ inversion)	*preposition + what* prép. + quoi est-ce-que prép. + quoi (+ inversion)

200

"WHICH (ONE), WHICH (ONES)"

There is another interrogative pronoun that we will examine because it does not follow the same pattern as the ones above.

IN ENGLISH

Which (one), which (ones) are used in questions that request the selection of one *(which one,* singular) or more than one *(which ones,* plural) from a group that has already been mentioned. The words *one* and *ones* are often omitted. These interrogative pronouns can refer to both persons and things and do not change according to function; they may be used as subjects, direct objects, indirect objects, and objects of a preposition.

210

> All the teachers are here. *Which one* teaches French?
>   group mentioned   singular subject

> I have two cars. *Which one* do you want to take?
>   group mentioned   singular direct object

> The library has many books. *Which ones* do you want?
>   group mentioned   plural direct object

220

> He has a group of friends. *Which ones* does he live with?
>   group mentioned   plural object of preposition *with*

IN FRENCH

As in English, these interrogative pronouns do not change according to function. However, their form changes in two ways:

1. their gender depends on the gender of their ANTECEDENT (i.e., the noun to which the pronoun refers), and

230

2. as in English. their number depends on whether you want to say *which **one*** (singular) or *which **ones*** (plural).

		MASCULINE	FEMININE
SINGULAR	*which (one)*	lequel	laquelle
PLURAL	*which (ones)*	lesquels	lesquelles

To choose the proper form, follow these steps:

1. Find the antecedent of *which.*
2. Determine the gender of the antecedent.

240

3. Do you wish to say *which one* → singular or *which ones* → plural?
4. Select the correct French form from the chart above.

Let us apply these steps to some examples.

All the books are here. ***Which one*** *is in French?*
1. Antecedent: the books
2. Gender: **Livres** *(books)* → masculine
3. Number: *one* → singular
4. Selection: masculine singular → **lequel**

250   Tous les livres sont ici. **Lequel** est en français?

I have two cars. ***Which one*** *do you want to take?*
1. Antecedent: the cars
2. Gender: **Voitures** *(cars)* → feminine
3. Number: *one* → singular
4. Selection: feminine singular → **laquelle**

J'ai deux voitures. **Laquelle** veux-tu prendre?

I have many books. ***Which ones*** *do you want to read?*
1. Antecedent: books
2. Gender: **Livres** *(books)* → masculine
260   3. Number: *ones* → plural
4. Selection: masculine plural → **lesquels**

J'ai beaucoup de livres. **Lesquels** veux-tu lire?

Here are four girls; ***which ones*** *do you want to speak* ***to?*** →
Here are four girls; ***to which ones*** *do you want to speak?*
1. Antecedent: girls
2. Gender: **Filles** *(girls)* → feminine
3. Number: *ones* → plural.
4. Selection: feminine plural → à + **lesquelles** → **auxquelles**

Voici quatre filles; **auxquelles** voulez-vous parler?

270   *There are two books.* ***Which one*** *are you speaking* ***about?*** →
There are two books. ***About which one*** *are you speaking?*
1. Antecedent: books
2. Gender: **Livres** *(books)* → masculine
3. Number: *one* → singular
4. Selection: masculine singular → **de** *(about)* + lequel → **duquel**

Il y a deux livres. **Duquel** parlez-vous?

STUDY TIPS — INTERROGATIVE PRONOUNS

Pattern (see *Tips for Learning Word Forms*, p. 4)
1. Look for a pattern that distinguishes the interrogative pronouns referring to people from those referring to things.

- PEOPLE — interrogative pronouns referring to people start with **qui** or preposition + **qui** (*Avec qui est-ce que tu étudies?*).
- THINGS — interrogative pronouns referring to things start with **qu'** or preposition + **quoi** (*Avec quoi est-ce que tu écris?*).

PERSON { Qui / Prep. + qui }   qui SUBJECT

est-ce

THING { Qu' / Prep. + quoi }   { que / qu' } OBJECT

2. Look for a pattern that distinguishes interrogative pronouns functioning as subjects from those functioning as objects.
   - SUBJECTS — interrogative pronoun subjects end in **qui**.
   - OBJECTS — interrogative pronoun objects end in **que (qu')**.
3. If you wish to learn the inversion forms, refer to the chart on p. 144. Remember that after the beginning **qui, qu'** or preposition + **qui/quoi**, you invert the subject pronoun and verb (*Avec qui étudies-tu?, Avec quoi écrivez-vous?*). EXCEPTION: If **qui** is the subject, it is followed by the verb (*Qui parle?, Qui est-ce qui parle?*).

Practice
1. On a blank piece of paper write questions using the various French forms.
2. Write French sentences answering "who," "what" questions. Then write a series of questions in French and answer them.

SENTENCE: L'étudiante lave la voiture avec du savon.

QUESTION: Qui lave la voiture?
ANSWER: L'étudiante lave la voiture.

QUESTION: Qu'est-ce que l'étudiante lave?
ANSWER: Elle lave la voiture.

QUESTION: Avec quoi est-ce qu'elle lave la voiture?
ANSWER: Elle lave la voiture avec du savon.

Flashcards
For review, create a card with a short question illustrating each form.

CHAPTER

43

WHAT IS A RELATIVE PRONOUN?

A **RELATIVE PRONOUN** is a word used at the beginning of a clause that gives additional information about someone or something previously mentioned.

relative clause
additional information about *the book*

I'm reading the book <u>*that* the teacher recommended</u>.

A relative pronoun serves two purposes:

1. It modifies a noun previously mentioned. The noun to which it refers is called the **ANTECEDENT**.

I saw the boy <u>*who* broke the window</u>.

antecedent of the relative pronoun *who*

2. It introduces a **RELATIVE CLAUSE,** a type of subordinate clause, that is, a group of words having a subject and a verb that cannot stand alone because it does not express a complete thought. A subordinate clause is dependent on a **MAIN CLAUSE;** that is, another group of words having a subject and a verb that can stand alone as a complete sentence because it expresses a complete thought. Relative clauses are underlined throughout the chapter; the remaining words correspond to the main clause.

The boy <u>*who broke the window*</u> *is very young.*

subject subject verb   verb

Relative clauses are very common. They allow us to combine in a single sentence two thoughts that have a common element.

SENTENCE A I met the teacher.
SENTENCE B He teaches French.
COMBINED I met the teacher <u>*who* teaches French</u>.

A relative pronoun can have different functions in the relative clause: subject, direct object, indirect object, or object of a preposition, or as a possessive relative pronoun. The relative pronoun used for each function often depends on whether its antecedent is a person (human being or animal) or a thing (objects, ideas). Some forms are more common in spoken English, others in formal or written English.

I. RELATIVE PRONOUN AS SUBJECT

(see *What is a Subject?*, p. 29)

IN ENGLISH

Relative pronouns functioning as subjects of a relative clause are always expressed in spoken and written English. The verb agrees with the antecedent of the relative pronoun and the relative pronoun used will depend on whether its antecedent is a person or a thing.

PERSON → *who* or *that*

> She is the student *who (that)* is learning French.
>
> antecedent   subject   verb
> 3rd per. sing.   person 3rd per. sing.

THING → *which* or *that*

> These are the books *which (that)* are so interesting.
>
> antecedent   subject   verb
> 3rd per. pl.   thing 3rd per. pl.

Combining sentences with a relative pronoun subject

> SENTENCE A   The students passed the exam.
> SENTENCE B   They studied.

1. Identify the common elements in sentences A and B.

   students and *they* = the same persons

2. The common element in Sentence A is the antecedent.

   students = antecedent

3. The common element in Sentence B is replaced by the relative pronoun.

   they → relative pronoun

4. The relative pronoun has the same function as the common element in Sentence B.

   they = subject of *studied* → relative pronoun = subject of *studied*

5. Choose the relative pronoun according to:
   a. its function (step 4)
   b. whether its antecedent (step 2) is a person or a thing

   they = subject referring to a person → *who* or *that*

6. Create the relative clause with relative pronoun (step 5) + remaining elements of Sentence B.

   who (that) studied

7. Place the relative clause right after its antecedent (step 2).

   > The students *who (that)* studied passed the exam.
   >
   > antecedent

IN FRENCH

There is only one relative pronoun used as subject of a relative clause → **qui** and the verb agrees with the antecedent of the relative pronoun.

*This is the student **who is learning French**.*
Voici l'étudiant **qui** apprend le français.

      antecedent   subject verb
      3rd per. sing. person 3rd per. sing.

*These are the books **that are so interesting**.*
Voici les livres **qui** sont si intéressants.

      antecedent   subject verb
      3rd per. pl. thing 3rd per. pl.

Combining sentences with a relative pronoun subject

Follow the steps under In English p. 149 (skip 5b).

SENTENCE A   Les étudiants ont réussi à l'examen.
                    The students passed the exam.

SENTENCE B   Ils ont étudié.
                    They studied.

Les étudiants **qui** ont étudié ont réussi à l'examen.
*The students **who studied** passed the exam.*

II. RELATIVE PRONOUN AS DIRECT OBJECT

(see p. 111 in *What is an Object?*)

IN ENGLISH

Relative pronouns functioning as direct objects are usually omitted in spoken English (in parentheses below). The relative pronoun used will depend on whether the antecedent is a person or a thing.

PERSON → (**whom, who,** or **that**)
      This is the student *(whom, who, that)* I saw yesterday.

            antecedent   direct object of *saw*

THING → (**that, which**)

      This is the book *(that, which)* Paul bought.

            antecedent   direct object of *bought*

Combining sentences with a relative pronoun direct object

Follow the steps under In English p. 149.

SENTENCE A The French teacher is nice.
SENTENCE B I met him yesterday.

1. Common elements: *French teacher* and *him*
2. Common element of sentence A: *French teacher* → antecedent
3. Common element of sentence B = *him* → relative pronoun
4. Function of *him*/relative pronoun: direct object of *met*
5. Relative pronoun: direct object person → *whom, who,* or *that*
6. Relative clause: *(whom, who, that)* + I met yesterday
7. Placement of relative clause: after *French teacher*

The French teacher <u>*(whom, who, that)* I met yesterday</u> is nice.

When the relative pronoun is omitted in spoken English ("The French teacher I met yesterday is nice") it is difficult to identify the two clauses.   130

IN FRENCH

Unlike in English, relative pronouns functioning as direct objects are never omitted. There is only one relative pronoun used as the direct object of a relative clause → **que** (**qu'** before a vowel).

> *This is the student **(whom, who, that)** I see often.*
> Voici l'étudiant **que** je vois souvent.
>
>   antecedent   direct object of **vois** *(see)*

> *This is the book **(that, which)** she is reading.*   140
> Voici le livre **qu'**elle lit.
>
>   antecedent direct object of **lit** *(is reading)*

Be sure to check on the type of object required by the French verb (see *Relationship of a verb to its object*, pp. 114-5).

Agreement of past participle: past participles conjugated with the auxiliary **avoir** agree with the direct object, if the direct object precedes the verb (see p. 65). In the case of relative clauses, the direct object relative pronoun **que** assumes the gender and number of the antecedent and the past participle must agree with it in gender and number.   150

> *These are the chairs **(that, which)** I bought.*
> Voici les chaises **que** j'ai achetées.
>
>   antecedent fem. pl. past participle fem. pl. (**acheté** + **es***)*

Combining sentences with a relative pronoun direct object

Follow the steps under In English (p. 149, skip 5b).

> SENTENCE A   Les étudiants parlent français.
>   *The students speak French.*
> SENTENCE B   J'ai vu les étudiants hier.
>   *I saw the students yesterday.*   160

> *The students **(that)** I saw yesterday speak French.*
> Les étudiants **que** j'ai vus hier parlent français.
>
> antecedent masc. pl. past participle masc. pl. (**vu** + **s**)

III. RELATIVE PRONOUN AS AN INDIRECT OBJECT AND OBJECT OF A PREPOSITION
(see p. 112 and p. 114 in *What is an Object?* and *What is a Preposition?*, p. 108)

IN ENGLISH

Relative pronouns functioning as indirect objects or objects of a preposition are usually omitted in spoken English (in parentheses below), but they are expressed in formal and written English right after the preposition. (See section below on restructuring sentences). The relative pronoun used will depend on whether the antecedent is a person or a thing.

PERSON → *(whom, who, that)* or preposition + *whom*

> I know the person *(whom, who, that)* he gave the book *to*. →
> I know the person *to whom* he gave the book.
>
>   antecedent   indirect object of *gave*

> Mary is the friend *(who, that)* I study *with*. →
> Mary is the friend *with whom* I study .
>
>   antecedent   object of preposition *with*

THING → *(that, which)* or preposition + *which*

> I know the museum *(that, which)* he gave the painting *to*? →
> I know the museum *to which* he gave the painting.
>
>   antecedent   indirect object of *gave*

Restructuring sentences with dangling prepositions (see p. 143-4)

To restructure spoken English to formal English, follow these steps:

1. Identify the antecedent.
2. Insert a relative pronoun after the antecedent.
3. Move the dangling preposition from the end of the clause (see pp. 142-3) and place it after the antecedent before the relative pronoun.

> Here is the student I was speaking *to*. →
> Here is the student *(who, that)* I was speaking *to*. →
> Here is the student *to whom* I was speaking.
>
>   antecedent   indirect object of *was speaking*

> The book I was speaking *about* is in French. →
> The book *(that, which)* I was speaking *about* is in French.→
> The book *about which* I was speaking is in French.
>
>   antecedent   object of preposition *about*

Combining sentences with a relative pronoun as an indirect object or as an object of a preposition

Follow the steps under In English, p. 149. Under step 6, move the preposition and place it before the relative pronoun.

SENTENCE A   The student has left.
SENTENCE B   I was speaking to him.

1. Common elements: *student* and *him*
2. Common element of sentence A: *student* → antecedent
3. Common element of sentence B: *him* → relative pronoun
4. Function of *him*/relative pronoun: indirect object of *was speaking (to)*
5. Relative pronoun: indirect object person → *whom*
6. Create relative clause (preposition + relative pronoun + remainder of sentence B): *to whom* I was speaking
7. Placement of relative clause: after *student*

Here is the student *to whom* I was speaking.

SENTENCE A   The book is interesting.
SENTENCE B   I was speaking about it.

1. Common elements: *book* and *it*
2. Common element of sentence A: *the book* → antecedent
3. Common element of sentence B: *it* → relative pronoun
4. Function of *it*/relative pronoun: object of preposition *about*
5. Relative pronoun: indirect object thing → *which*
6. Create relative clause (preposition + relative pronoun + remainder of sentence B): *about which* I was speaking
7. Placement relative clause: after *book*

The book *about which* I was speaking is interesting.

IN FRENCH

Unlike in English, relative pronouns functioning as indirect objects and as objects of a preposition are never omitted and follow the structure of formal English. These relative pronouns are divided into two groups according to the preposition required by the French verb or expression: 1. relative pronouns as objects of a preposition other than the preposition **de** 2. relative pronouns as object of the preposition **de**. Be sure to check on the type of object required by the French verb (see *Relationship of a verb to its object*, pp. 114-5).

1. FRENCH RELATIVE PRONOUNS AS OBJECTS OF A PREPOSITION OTHER THAN THE PREPOSITION "DE"

This group includes French verbs followed by the preposition **à** *(to)* which introduces indirect objects and all prepositions except the preposition **de** *(of, about*, etc.). As in formal English, the relative clause always begins with the preposition followed by a relative pronoun. The relative pronoun used will depend on whether the antecedent is a person or a thing.

PERSON → preposition + **qui**

*Here is the man **(who, that) I am talking to**.* →
*Here is the man **to whom** I am talking.* →
Voici l'homme **à qui** je parle.

210

220

230

240

250

THING → preposition + **lequel** which agrees with the antecedent in gender and number (see pp. 145-6)

These are the pens (that, which) I write with. →
These are the pens with which I write.
Voici les stylos **avec lesquels** j'écris.
          | |
      masc. pl.   masc. pl.

260

In addition, following the preposition **à** *(to)* the initial **le-** and **les-** become **au-** and **aux-**.

These are the rules (that, which) we obey.→
                            |
                 to obey→ **obéir à**
These are the rules to which we obey.
Voici les règles **auxquelles** nous obéissons.
          | |
     fem. pl.   à + fem. pl. **(lesquelles)** → **auxquelles**

Combining sentences with a relative pronoun as indirect object or object of a preposition other than "de"

270

Follow the steps under In English, p. 149. Under step 6, use the preposition required by the French verb at the beginning of the relative clause.

SENTENCE A   Il connaît la dame.
                    He knows the lady.
SENTENCE B   Je parle à la dame.
                    I speak to the lady.
Il connaît la dame **à qui** je parle.
He knows the lady to whom I speak.
                       |
                 indirect object

280

SENTENCE A   La table est solide.
                    The table is solid.
SENTENCE B   Il travaille sur la table.
                    He works on the table.
La table **sur laquelle** il travaille est solide.
     | |
  fem. sing.   fem. sing.
The table on which he works is solid.
             |
     object of preposition *on*

2. FRENCH RELATIVE PRONOUNS AS OBJECTS OF THE PREPOSITION "DE"

290

This group includes French verbs or expressions followed by the preposition **de**. The relative pronoun **dont** replaces the preposition **de** and its object which can refer to either a person or a thing. **Dont** is placed at the beginning of the relative clause.

*The course **(that, which)** I am talking **about*** is difficult. →
*The course **about which I am talking*** is difficult.

       replaces *course*   to talk about → **parler de**
Le cours **dont je parle** est difficile.

   replaces **du cours**

Combining sentences with a relative pronoun object of the preposition "de"

300

Follow the steps under In English, p. 149 (skip 5b).

SENTENCE A: Voici le professeur.
               Here is the teacher.
SENTENCE B: Je me souviens de lui.
               I remember him.

*Here is the teacher **(whom, who, that)** I remember.*

                    to remember → **se souvenir de**
Voici le professeur **dont je me souviens.**

310

         replaces **de lui**

IV. POSSESSIVE RELATIVE PRONOUN "WHOSE"
IN ENGLISH

The English relative pronoun *whose* indicates that the antecedent is the possessor of the noun that follows. It can refer to a person or a thing .

     This is the boy *whose* mother I know.

         the boy's mother → the mother *of the boy* → whose mother
     I know the house *whose* roof burned.

320

        the house's roof → the roof *of the house* → whose roof

IN FRENCH

The equivalent of *whose* is **dont** which can refer to a person or a thing.

SENTENCE A: *This is the boy.*
               Voici le garçon.
SENTENCE B: *I know his mother. → I know the mother of the boy.*
               Je connais sa mère. → Je connais la mère du garçon.

*This is the boy **whose mother I know**.*

330

Voici le garçon **dont je connais la mère**.

SENTENCE A: *Look at the house.*
               Regardez la maison.
SENTENCE B: *The roof of the house burned.*
               Le toit de la maison a brûlé.

*Look at the house **whose roof burned**.*
Regardez la maison **dont** le toit a brulé.

SUMMARY OF RELATIVE PRONOUNS WITH AN ANTECEDENT

Here is a chart you can use as reference:

FUNCTION IN RELATIVE CLAUSE:	ANTECEDENT	
	PERSON	THING
SUBJECT	*who, that* **qui**	*which, that* **qui**
DIRECT OBJECT	*(whom, who, that)* **que**	*(that, which)* **que**
INDIRECT OBJECT & OBJECT OF PREPOSITION OTHER THAN "DE"	*preposition* *+ whom* **prép. + qui**	*preposition* *+ which* **prép. + lequel**
OBJECT OF PREPOSITION "DE"	*preposition* *+ whom* **dont**	*preposition* *+ which* **dont**
POSSESSIVE	*whose* **dont**	*whose* **dont**

To find the appropriate French relative pronoun, go through the following steps:

1. Restructure the English clause if there is a dangling preposition.
   - Add the relative pronoun, if it has been omitted.
2. To choose the French relative pronoun, establish the function of the relative pronoun in the French relative clause.
   - If the relative pronoun is the subject → **qui**.
   - If the French verb takes a direct object → **que** or **qu'**. If the French verb has a past participle conjugated with **avoir**, make sure the past participle agrees with the antecedent, see p. 151.
   - If the French verb is followed by a preposition other than **de**: if a person → preposition + **qui**; if a thing → preposition + appropriate form of **lequel**.
   - If the French verb or expression is followed by the preposition **de** → **dont**.
3. Placement after the antecedent:
   - If the relative pronoun is the subject or the direct object → relative pronoun + clause
   - If the relative pronoun is the object of a preposition other than **de** → the preposition + relative pronoun + clause
   - If the relative pronoun is the object of the preposition **de** → **dont** + clause

Let us apply the steps above to the following sentences:

*The plane **(that, which)** comes from Paris is late.*
    1. Relative clause: that comes from Paris
    2. Function of the relative pronoun: subject → **qui**
    3. Antecedent: *plane* (**avion**)
    4. Placement: antecedent (**avion**) + **qui** + clause
L'avion **qui** arrive de Paris est en retard.

*Here are the books **(that, which)** I bought yesterday.*
    1. Relative clause: that I bought yesterday   390
    2. Function of the relative pronoun: direct object of **acheter** *(to buy)* → **que**
    3. Antecedent: *books* (**livres** = masc. pl.)
    4. Placement: antecedent (**livres**) + **que** + clause
    5. Agreement of past participle: **achetés** (masc. pl.)
Voici les livres **que** j'ai achetés hier.

*That is the boy **(whom, who, that)** she is playing with.* →
*That is the boy **with whom she is playing**.*
    1. Relative clause: with whom she is playing
    2. Function of the relative pronoun: object of the preposition **avec** *(with)* + person *(boy)* → **avec qui**   400
    3. Antecedent: *boy* (**garçon**)
    4. Placement: antecedent (**garçon**) + **avec qui** + clause
Voici le garçon **avec qui** elle joue.

*Where is the table **(that, which)** he's working on?* →
*Where is the table **on which he's working**?*
    1. Relative clause: on which he is working
    2. Function of the relative pronoun: object of preposition **sur** *(on)* + thing *(table)*
    3. Antecedent: *table* (**table** = feminine singular)
    4. Placement: antecedent (**table**) + **sur laquelle** + clause   410
Où est la table **sur laquelle** il travaille?

*Where is the book **(that, which)** you need?*
    1. Relative clause: that you need
    2. Function of the relative pronoun: object of preposition **de** *(to need → **avoir besoin de**)*
    3. Selection: **dont**
    4. Antecedent: *book* (**livre**)
    5. Placement: antecedent (**livre**) + **dont** + clause
Où est le livre **dont** vous avez besoin?

Relative pronouns can be tricky. Refer to your French textbook for additional explanations and rules.   420

RELATIVE PRONOUNS WITHOUT AN ANTECEDENT

There are relative pronouns that do not refer to a specific noun or pronoun. Instead, they refer to an antecedent that has not been expressed or to an entire idea.

IN ENGLISH

Some relative pronouns can be used without an antecedent: *what, which, that.*

430
- to refer to an unspecified thing or event → *what*

    I don't know <u>what</u> happened.
        no antecedent
        subject

    Here is <u>what</u> I read.
        no antecedent
        direct object

- to refer to an entire idea, expressed in a preceding clause → comma + *which* or *that*

440
    She didn't do well, <u>which</u> is a pity.
        antecedent: the fact that she didn't do well
        subject of *is*

    To speak French well, <u>that</u> is what I want.
        antecedent: the fact that the person wants to speak French well
        subject of *is*

CAREFUL — Don't confuse the relative pronoun *what* with other uses of *what*: as an interrogative pronoun, see p. 141 (***What** do you want?* **Qu'est-ce que** vous voulez?), and as an interrogative adjective, see p. 99 (***What** book do you want?* **Quel** livre voulez-vous?).

450

IN FRENCH

When a relative pronoun does not have a specific antecedent or refers to an idea, the pronoun **ce** *(that)* is added to act as the antecedent. It is followed by the relative pronoun appropriate to its function in the relative clause.

Here are a few examples.

    *Here is **what happened**.*
460
    1. Relative clause: what happened
    2. No antecedent: add **ce**
    3. Function: subject of **est arrivé** *(happened)* → **ce qui**
    Voici <u>**ce qui** est arrivé</u>.

*He doesn't speak French, **which** will be a problem.*
    1. Relative clause: which will be a problem
    2. Antecedent: "he doesn't speak French" → add **ce**
    3. Function: subject of **sera** *(will be)* → **ce qui**

Il ne parle pas français, **ce qui** sera un problème.

*Show me **what** you bought.*
    1. Relative clause: what you bought
    2. No antecedent: add **ce**
    3. Function: direct object of **avez acheté** *(bought)* → **ce que**   470

Montrez-moi **ce que** vous avez acheté.

*I don't know **what** he is talking about.*
    1. Relative clause: *what* he is talking *about* →
       Restructured: *about what* he is talking
    2. No antecedent: add **ce**
    3. Function: object of preposition **de** *(to speak about* →
       parler de) → **ce dont**

Je ne sais pas **ce dont** il parle.

CHAPTER

WHAT IS A DEMONSTRATIVE PRONOUN?

A **DEMONSTRATIVE PRONOUN** is a word that replaces a noun as if pointing to it. The word *demonstrative* comes from *demonstrate*, to show.

Choose a suit. *This one* is expensive. *That one* is not.
antecedent points to one suit   points to another suit

In English and in French demonstrative pronouns can be used in a variety of ways.

"THIS ONE, THAT ONE" AND "THESE, THOSE"

IN ENGLISH

The singular demonstrative pronouns are **this (one)** and **that (one)**; the plural forms are **these** and **those**.

Here are my suitcases. *This one* is big ; *those* are small.
antecedent   singular   plural

Choose a book. *Those* are in French, *that one* is in English.
antecedent   plural   singular

This (one), *these* refer to persons or things near the speaker, and *that (one)*, *those* refer to persons or things further away from the speaker.

IN FRENCH

Demonstrative pronouns agree in gender with their **ANTECEDENT**; that is, the noun to which they refer. Their number depends on whether they refer to one person or thing *(this one, that one)* or to more than one person or thing *(these, those)*. Also, **-ci** is added to indicate persons or things close to the speaker and **-là** to indicate persons or things further away.

		MASCULINE	FEMININE
SINGULAR	*this, that (one)*	celui-ci, celui-là	celle-ci, celle-là
PLURAL	*these, those*	ceux-ci, ceux-là	celles-ci, celles-là

To choose the correct form, follow these steps:

1. Find the antecedent.
2. Determine the gender of the antecedent.

3. Number: *this one, that one* → singular; *these, those* → plural.
4. Based on steps 2 and 3 choose the correct form from the chart on p. 160.
5. Add **-ci** for *this* or *these* and **-là** for *that* and *those*.

Look at the following examples.

*Which book did you read? **This one.***
Quel livre as-tu lu? **Celui-ci.**
1. Antecedent: book
2. Gender: **Livre** *(book)* → masculine
3. Number: *This one* → singular
4. Selection: **celui**
5. *This* → **-ci**

*Which letter did you read? **That one.***
Quelle lettre as-tu lue? **Celle-là.**
1. Antecedent: letter
2. Gender: **Lettre** *(letter)* → feminine
3. Number: *That one* → singular
4. Selection: **celle**
5. *That* → **-là**

*Which books did you read? **These.***
Quels livres as-tu lus? **Ceux-ci.**
1. Antecedent: books
2. Gender: **Livres** *(books)* → masculine
3. Number: *These* → plural
4. Selection: **ceux**
5. *These* → **-ci**

*Which letters did you read? **Those.***
Quelles lettres as-tu lues? **Celles-là.**
1. Antecedent: letters
2. Gender: **Lettres** *(letters)* → feminine
3. Number: *Those* → plural
4. Selection: **celles**
5. *Those* → **-là**

TO SHOW POSSESSION: "CELUI DE" (see also *What is the Possessive?*, p. 22)

IN ENGLISH

You can show possession with an apostrophe after the possessor, without repeating the person or thing possessed mentioned in a previous sentence. The person or thing possessed is the antecedent.

Do you have a car? No, I use my *father's*.
             | |
   antecedent   possessor + apostrophe

The word *car* is not repeated after *father*; it is understood.

IN FRENCH

Remember that the apostrophe structure to show possession does not exist in French (see p. 23). For the same reason that "my father's house" can only be expressed with the structure "the house *of* my father," the expression "my father's" can only be expressed with a structure that does not require an apostrophe. This structure word-for-word corresponds to "the one of" (singular antecedent) or "the ones of" (plural antecedent).

Do you have a car? No, I'm using my father's.

antecedent   possessor + apostrophe
singular   *"the one of* my father"

Do you have your keys? No, I'm using my father's.

antecedent   possessor + apostrophe
plural   *"the ones of* my father"

To show possession when the person or thing possessed is not stated in the same sentence, French uses the demonstrative pronouns (without -**ci** or -**là**) + **de** *(of)*.

To choose the correct form, follow these steps:

1. Find the antecedent of *"the one"* or *"the ones."*
2. Determine the gender and number of the antecedent.
3. Based on step 2, select the form of the demonstrative pronoun on the chart p. 160.
4. Add the preposition **de** *(of)*.

Let us apply these rules to the following examples:

Which house are you selling? **My father's.**

antecedent   *"the one of my father"*

Quelle maison vendez-vous? **Celle de** mon père.
1. Antecedent: *house* (**maison**)
2. Gender & number: **maison** *(house)* → feminine singular
3. Demonstrative pronoun: **celle**
4. Selection: **celle de**

Which books are you taking? **The young man's.**

antecedent   *"the ones of the young man"*

Quels livres prenez-vous? **Ceux du** jeune homme.
1. Antecedent: *books* (**livres**)
2. Gender & number: **livres** *(books)* → masculine plural
3. Demonstrative pronoun: **ceux**
4. Selection: **ceux de**

"THE ONE (THAT)": **"CELUI QUI, CELUI QUE"** (see *What is a Relative Pronoun?*, p. 148)

120

IN ENGLISH

The pronouns *the one* (singular antecedent) and *the ones* (plural antecedent), followed by the relative pronouns *that, which,* or *who,* can start a relative clause giving us additional information about a person or thing mentioned in a previous sentence. Since the relative pronouns *that, which,* or *who* are often omitted in English, we have indicated them between parentheses.

What book are you reading? *The one (that)* you gave me.
Clause: *the one that you gave me =*
additional information about *the book*
Number: *The one* is singular.

130

Which girls went to Paris? *The ones (who)* spoke French.
Clause: *the ones who spoke French =*
additional information about *the girls*
Number: *The ones* is plural.

IN FRENCH

To express the English structure above, French uses the demonstrative pronouns followed by a relative pronoun.

140

- The demonstrative pronouns agree in gender and number with the antecedent.
- The relative pronoun is selected according to its function in the relative clause.

To choose the correct form, follow these steps:

A. Demonstrative pronoun *(the one, the ones)*
1. Find the antecedent.
2. Determine the gender and number of the antecedent.
3. Select the French form according to the chart on p. 160.

B. Relative pronoun *(that, which, who—add to the English sentence if it has been omitted)*

150

1. Determine the function of the relative pronoun in the relative clause.
2. Select the correct French form based on step 1:
   - subject → **qui**
   - object → **que**

Let us apply these rules to the following examples:

What books are you reading? **The ones (that)** *you gave me.*
A. Demonstrative pronoun *(the ones)*
1. Antecedent: books **(livres)**
2. Gender & number: **livres** *(books)* → masculine plural
3. Selection: **ceux**

160

B. Relative pronoun *(that)*
 1. Function: *that* is the object of the relative clause.
  (Answers the question: "You gave *what?*" *You* is the subject.)
 2. Selection: **que**

Quels livres lis-tu? **Ceux que** tu m'as donnés.

antecedent	dem. pronoun + relative pronoun	
masc. pl.	masc. pl.	object

Note: The past participle **donnés** agrees with the direct object **livres** (masc. pl.) which precedes it (see pp. 65 & 151).

*Which girls went to Paris? **The ones who** spoke French.*
 A. Demonstrative pronoun *(the ones)*
  1. Antecedent: girls **(filles)**
  2. Gender & number: **filles** *(girls)* → feminine plural
  3. Selection: **celles**
 B. Relative pronoun *(who)*
  1. Function: *who* is the subject of the relative clause.
  2. Selection: **qui**

Quelles filles sont allées à Paris ? **Celles qui** parlaient français.

antecedent	dem. pronoun + relative pronoun	
fem. pl.	fem. pl.	subject

WHAT IS MEANT BY ACTIVE
AND PASSIVE VOICE?

VOICE in the grammatical sense refers to the relationship between the verb and its subject. There are two voices, the **ACTIVE VOICE** and the **PASSIVE VOICE**.

ACTIVE VOICE — A sentence is said to be in the active voice when the subject is the performer of the action of the verb. In this instance, the verb is called an **ACTIVE VERB**.

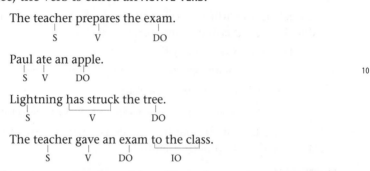

The teacher prepares the exam.
    S   V   DO

Paul ate an apple.
 S   V   DO

Lightning has struck the tree.
    S   V   DO

The teacher gave an exam to the class.
    S   V   DO   IO

In all these examples the subject (S) performs the action of the verb (V) and the direct object (DO) or the indirect object (IO) is the receiver of the action (see *What is a Subject?*, p. 29 and *What is an Object?*, p.111).

PASSIVE VOICE — A sentence is said to be in the passive voice when the subject is the receiver of the action of the verb. In this instance, the verb is called a **PASSIVE VERB**.

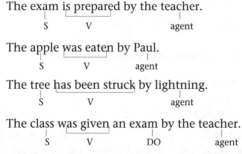

The exam is prepared by the teacher.
    S   V   agent

The apple was eaten by Paul.
    S   V   agent

The tree has been struck by lightning.
    S   V   agent

The class was given an exam by the teacher.
    S   V   DO   agent

In all these examples, the subject is the receiver of the action of the verb. The performer of the action, if it is mentioned, is introduced by the word "by" and is called the **AGENT**.

IN ENGLISH

The passive voice is expressed by the auxiliary verb *to be* conjugated in the different tenses + the past participle of the main verb (see p. 61 in *What is a Participle?*). The tense of the passive sentence is indicated by the tense of the verb *to be*.

> The exam ***is** prepared* by the teacher.
> 　　　｜　　｜
> 　　　S　present

> The exam ***was** prepared* by the teacher.
> 　　　　　｜
> 　　　　past

> The exam ***will be** prepared* by the teacher.
> 　　　｜＿＿＿｜
> 　　　future

A direct or an indirect object of the verb can function as the subject of the passive sentence.

> The *exam* was given by the teacher.
> 　　｜
> 　　S (the teacher gave *the exam* → DO in the active sentence)

> The students were given *an exam.*
> 　　　｜
> 　　　S (the exam was given *to the students* → IO in the active sentence)

While the use of the passive voice is very common in English, it is often avoided in French.

IN FRENCH

As in English, a passive verb is expressed with the auxiliary **être** (*to be*) conjugated in the appropriate tense + the past participle of the main verb. The tense of the passive sentence is indicated by the tense of the verb **être**.

> L'examen **est** préparé par le professeur.
> 　　　　｜
> 　　　present
> *The exam **is** prepared by the teacher.*

> L'examen **a été** préparé par le professeur.
> 　　　　｜＿＿｜
> 　　　　past
> *The exam **has been (was)** prepared by the teacher.*

> L'examen **sera** préparé par le professeur.
> 　　　　｜
> 　　　future
> *The exam **will be** prepared by the teacher.*

Since past participles of passive verbs are always conjugated with the auxiliary **être**, the past participles of passive verbs always agree in gender and number with the subject (see p. 64).

Les vins français sont **appréciés** dans le monde entier.   80
subject → masc. pl.   past participle → masc. pl.
*French **wines** are **appreciated** the world over.*

Unlike in English, only the direct object of a verb in an active sentence can function as the subject of a French passive sentence. When the object of the verb is indirect, the passive voice is avoided by using the **on** construction below (see p. 168).

AVOIDING THE PASSIVE VOICE IN FRENCH

If the agent is mentioned, a passive sentence is turned into   90
an active sentence.

1. The agent of the passive sentence introduced with *by* becomes the subject of the active sentence and the subject of passive sentence is made the direct object of the active sentence.

> PASSIVE   ***The exam** is prepared **by the teacher**.*
>   S   agent
> ACTIVE   ***The teacher** prepares **the exam**.*
>   S   DO
>   **Le professeur** prépare **l'examen**.   100

2. The tense of the verb *to be* in the passive sentence is reflected in the active sentence.

> PASSIVE   *The exam **is** prepared by the teacher.*
> (PRESENT)
> ACTIVE   *The teacher **prepares** the exam.*
> PRÉSENT   Le professeur **prépare** l'examen.

> PASSIVE   *The exam **was** prepared by the teacher.*
> (PAST)
> ACTIVE   *The teacher **prepared** the exam.*   110
> PASSÉ COMPOSÉ   Le professeur **a préparé** l'examen.

> PASSIVE   *The exam **will be** prepared by the teacher.*
> (FUTURE)
> ACTIVE   *The teacher **will prepare** the exam.*
> FUTUR   Le professeur **préparera** l'examen.

If the agent is not mentioned in the passive sentence, there are two possible constructions to avoid the passive.

1. REFLEXIVE VERB CONSTRUCTION — The main verb of the sen-   120
tence is changed to a reflexive verb (see *What are Reflexive Pronouns and Verbs?*, p. 131). This reflexive construction is used primarily for general statements.

Coats are worn in the winter.
Les manteaux se portent en hiver.

The New York Times is sold here.
Le New York Times se vend ici.

2. "ON" CONSTRUCTION — The pronoun **on** is added to serve as the subject of an active sentence. In this instance, **on** corresponds to the English indefinite pronoun *one,* as in the sentence, *"One should eat when one is hungry."*

> *English is taught in many universities.*
> > *English,* the subject, is not doing the teaching;
> > therefore, the sentence is in the passive voice.
> **On enseigne** l'anglais dans beaucoup d'universités.
> > **On,** the subject, is doing the teaching;
> > therefore, the sentence is in the active voice.

> *French was spoken in class.*
> > *French,* the subject, was not doing the speaking;
> > therefore, the sentence is in the passive voice.
> **On parlait** français en classe.
> > **On,** the subject, was doing the speaking;
> > therefore, the sentence is in the active voice.

In addition, the pronoun **on** is added to serve as the subject of an active sentence in order to avoid a passive sentence with an indirect object as subject.

> PASSIVE   ***The children** were given presents.*
> > S (presents were given *to the children* → IO in active sentence)

> ACTIVE   **On** a donné des cadeaux aux enfants.
> > S [word-for-word: *one* gave presents to the children]

CAREFUL — Remember that in the active voice verbs form their past tenses with either **être** *(to be)* or **avoir** *(to have)* as auxiliary (see p. 47). French verbs that form their past tenses with the auxiliary **être** in the active voice cannot be made passive.